I Need Therapy

I Need Therapy

Glenda Wallace

Pink Kiss Publishing Company
Gautier, Mississippi

To protect the privacy of the parties involved, no real names or precise fact patterns have been used in this work.

Dedication

This book is dedicated to my mother, Mary Smith.
You are my inspiration.

Acknowledgments

The best thing about my life is all of the wonderful people who are in it. Not a day goes by that I don't feel blessed to have so many wonderful supportive family and friends in my circle.

I always want to give a very special thanks to the love of my life, Seymour Greenidge-Blake, for his undying love and for being my biggest supporter. Above all, I thank you for your patience.

Thanks to my mom, Mary Smith, for always being my biggest inspiration.

To the rest of my extended family and friends, I love you all, thanks for your support.

I have to thank the fabulous team of people that made this book happen:

Donna Clark, my graphic artist for all the hard work and patience she put in over the years. Once again your cover is on point lady.

Brenda Lewis, my interior book designer, for producing awesome interior layouts.

Autumn Conley Bittick, one of the best editors I know. You are a lifesaver! For whatever errors and inaccuracies which may still exist, I take full responsibility. You know I'm always adding and subtracting from what is supposed to be the finished product. Thank you ladies!

Last but definitely not least, to my Lord and Savior Jesus Christ, the head of my life. Thank you for always shining your favor on me!

X

CONTENTS

Why Therapy?

My man has been and always will be the king of my castle. I pamper him and place him on a pedestal. When I'm in love with him, I will do *anything* for him, and that is as it should be, but ladies, we know how easy it is to fall out of love — or should I say, to be *pushed* out of love? Unfortunately, these same ideas and high opinions some of us have of our men can also eventually be perceived by that man, our king, as a weakness.

Some men don't know how to handle a woman's heart, and they can become neglectful and unappreciative. Sadly, some of them are not even aware they are committing this injustice. Sometimes, a man may view his woman's efforts to please him and keep him satisfied as being weak and needy; men can be and often are intimidated by strong-minded, independent women. Face it, ladies … a man will always be a man. Throughout my lifetime, whenever I've become unhappy with one man's faults and decided I could not and would not live with those faults, I simply moved on to the next man, the next *new* relationship. But unfortunately, the next man came with his own set of faults, and the cycle continued. Looking for a good man is a process, and there will be many misfires along the way.

To find a good man, we must determine what a *good man* really is. What qualities make him a good man? Ladies, we must decide individually for ourselves what that means. In relationships, women want a man who is the total package. We look for companionship. We want a man who is a great provider and has the ability to give us great sex. We want our man to be our best friend and soul mate. Can all of these qualities really be found in one man? I would like to think so, but let's face it, probably not. It is all too common to find a man who is great in one area but lacking in another. If, for example, he is a great provider and father, he may not be exciting in the bed-room. Maybe he works long hours in order to be a great provider, but then he doesn't have enough time or energy left to think about romance. I have heard many women say that if we could take the best characteristic from each man and combine them, we would have the perfect man. That might be so in a perfect world, but in the real world, we must take what we have and work with it.

Although I have never believed in cheating in a relationship or marriage, I do feel women cheat for different reasons than men. Some men cheat simply based on the physical characteristics of a woman. Since men are naturally visually stimulated, a nice body and a pretty face is reason enough for some to cheat. Women, on the other hand, typically cheat based on emotions. Women crave emotional stimulation in our relationships. When we don't get that from the man in our life, we will find it in someone else.

Most women will admit to having a *standby*. A standby is someone who is ready and waiting to step in at any given moment if anything should happen to go wrong in your current relationship. He may be a friend, a coworker, or someone who is close enough to you that you feel comfortable enough to confide in him. He is normally so into you that he pays attention to details. He will be the first one to remember your birthday, often even before your man does. He listens to your wants and needs, and he waits. He tunes in to what you are missing in your current relationship, so he knows exactly what you need. Your standby will be whatever you want him to be. He will comfort you when you need comforting. He will be your best friend and lend an ear when you need him to listen. He will even be your lover. He will offer you all that you are lacking in your current relationship, but he *will* be there when you are most vulnerable and need a shoulder to cry on. Women won't normally fall in love with a standby, but we will use him as the rebound guy, the one who helps us get over the man we love who has broken our hearts. We use our standby to feed our ego. We enjoy the attention he gives us and the boost to our self-esteem. Normally, the standby is who we allow to feed our emotional side.

In addition to our standby, we also have each other. Women share a common bond. At some point in our lives, we have all been hurt by a man. It does not matter how pretty or how skinny you are, for skinny girls get hurt just like the big girls. Some of the most beautiful women in the world have been betrayed in a relationship. It is inconsequential how much money you make or your social background, as we have all been hurt at some point in time. So, when you are going through emotional heartache, know that you are not alone. What is important is how you handle that heartache.

When we are hurt by a man, there are a number of things we must do in order to keep our sanity. There is no weakness in crying or showing anger. Cry, throw things, and do whatever it takes to get it out of your system. Crying and displaying anger is a natural part of the recovery process. Recognize that grieving is essential to healing, and it is okay to grieve when you lose someone you love. Then pick yourself up and begin healing. I don't care if you have eight kids and weigh 300 pounds. You must begin healing by embracing the beauty in you — and there *is* beauty in you, whether you see it or not.

We relate to movies and stories that deal with infidelity because, for most women, when we have been hurt by a man, we indulge in overeating, excessive alcohol consumption, and negative thinking; all self-destructive behaviors. When we listen to the lyrics of some of our favorite songs, we know that someone actually lived that pain and hurt that we hear in those lyrics — and it is a pain most of us can relate to.

When a man leaves us for another woman, we have a habit of beating ourselves up. We convince ourselves that it is our fault he left, our fault that he cheated. We look at the other woman and ask ourselves, *what does she have that I don't?* We make excuses, *if I had done this differently, then maybe he would have stayed.* Ladies, when a man lies and cheats, it is NOT your fault! It doesn't mean you have done anything wrong. We are quick to blame ourselves, but we are not responsible for the choices our men make. What hurts a man most is when he sees that his behavior has not crippled us. When men leave us, cheat on us, or put us in a position where we are forced to leave them because of their lies and deceit, they draw strength from our suffering. They feel power when they see that we can't go on without them, but ladies, we CAN go on! We are the powerful ones!

After a breakup, you must begin to take control of your life by taking care of someone you've probably been neglecting — YOU! The greatest weapon and the sweetest revenge is a smile. When a man breaks up with you, he expects you to be miserable without him. Don't give him the satisfaction! Throw back your shoulders, put a smile on your face, and face the world with confidence, even if you're not really feeling it and you are only putting on a façade. When you are out in public around friends and family, act as though you are happier without him than you ever were with him. You'd better believe that after a breakup, everyone around you — especially mutual friends and coworkers — will be watching to see how you are coping. Some will even take comfort in your misery, but you simply can't give anyone that much power over you. What hurts a man most is when someone says to him, "I saw your ex and Man, she was looking good. She was smiling and looked happy." When a relationship ends men expect us to have an emotional breakdown, and when we don't, they don't know how to interpret our lack of emotion. The tears will probably come, and crying is okay, but save those tears for those private moments when you are behind closed doors.

After a breakup is the perfect time for a change, so use this time for healing and self-love. Know that you have the power to make some positive changes in your life, and that includes letting go of any negative energy you are holding onto from past relationships. Take the focus off of him and put it on you. True happiness doesn't come from a relationship you have with a man, it begins with the relationship you have with yourself. If your man has done something that hurt you and the relationship is over, rejoice and be thankful. Your daily anthem should read, "Lord, I was happy with me before I ever met that man and I'm even happier with me now!" If you're not happy with you, make a commitment to *be* happy with you. Find ways to be good to yourself and start loving yourself again.

When healing from a breakup, it is important to make yourself feel as attractive as possible to boost your own level of confidence. Even though your romantic relationship is over you still have to nurture that relationship you have with you, so learn to have a love affair with yourself. A spa day is a great way to pamper you. Treat yourself to a massage, and get a complete makeover, maybe get a new hair cut or a new color. Go shopping and buy a new wardrobe. If you can afford it, you should even go all out and indulge yourself in a big way by taking a trip to that exotic island you've been thinking about. This could be the perfect opportunity to get your girlfriends together for that singles cruise.

Part of taking care of you means taking care of your body and your health. Join a gym. Working out conditions not only the body, but the mind as well and it is a great way to relieve stress. When you are physically fit, not only does it improve your overall health and well-being by making you feel stronger and healthier, but your overall appearance will improve. Being physically fit also assists with self-esteem issues. It is a known fact that when you feel good, you look good. As an added bonus, the gym is a great place to meet single, attractive men. If we condition our minds that certain types of male behavior is not good for us; for our health and well-being, we can then provide therapy for ourselves and for our souls.

I embark upon this journey full of personal experiences of not only myself, but those of female friends, family, coworkers and neighbors of all races, cultures, and national origins. I began my journey at the age of nineteen with my first intimate relationship with a man. Now, at age 44, after five marriages and eighteen proposals, I can truly say that I have evolved.

In my quest to show the strength of the common bonds of sisterhood shared by women, I encouraged women to speak out and share their experiences about men, love and relationships. I believe we can all learn from each other. By sharing our stories, we can bond together, provide support, and encourage one another to find strength while facing our life challenges. During the interview process for this book, I wanted to know which issues women viewed as the most important in their relationships. The majority felt *security* was of utmost importance, whether it was financial, emotional, or spiritual. I asked women from all over the world,

"What is the one thing that would completely destroy your faith in your relationship?" The answers were:

- ✴ Cheating
- ✴ Physical, verbal, and/or emotional abuse
- ✴ Lying
- ✴ Not providing for the family
- ✴ Lack of or no communication
- ✴ Lack of intimacy

I personally view lying and cheating as one in the same. There is nothing worse than a lying man, and I have ended numerous relationships for the lies that men have told me, no matter how insignificant. I feel that if a man will lie, he will also cheat. But I have decided to accept the fact that men cannot help the way that they are; they experience a male version of PMS. Men relate to everyday issues on a totally different level than women. Although men and women have different views on relationship issues, there is no excuse for dishonesty.

As women, we must never let a man bring our spirits down. Always make yourself as attractive as possible. When you *feel* attractive, you *are* attractive. You have attitude. When you feel attractive, it shows. We have all seen television shows like *The Swan* and *Extreme Makeovers* where ordinary women for various different reasons are not happy with themselves or their physical appearances. They suffer from low self-esteem and ask to be transformed. Before the so-called 'miraculous transformations', the women are just ordinary, but after the transformation she is beautiful, sexy, and confident.

She immediately has attitude, and she is beautiful.

I am not suggesting that in order to feel confident about yourself, you must go through the extreme of plastic surgery, but there are other changes you can make to develop and achieve self-confidence. Years ago, one of my best girlfriends had the worst self-esteem problem. She weighed 290 pounds, wore huge, thick-rimmed glasses, and had short, unattractive hair. She always wore homely clothes that were big, baggy and hung off her body. She dressed like that because she was trying to disguise her weight. One day she said to me that she wished she was thin and pretty like me because maybe then men would notice her. I told her that there is nothing special about me. By no means am I extraordinarily beautiful, but I disguise the fact that I am quite ordinary by being confident, approach-able, and I play up my assets. All women have assets. The important thing is learning how to identify your assets, which we will cover in a later chapter.

Over the years, I taught myself to be sexy. For years, I had been interviewing men in order to find out what captures their attention in a woman, asking them about their greatest desires. I told my friend she was unattractive because she *believed* she was unat-tractive. Actually, in many ways, she was a very beauti-ful girl. She had gorgeous brown eyes with the longest, thickest lashes. Many women have invested thousands of dollars in Maybelline mascara just to get that look that she possessed naturally. Yet, no one could see how beautiful her eyes were because of the glasses. She also had a beautiful smile and a slamming personality. She just didn't know how to display her assets to her benefit. I showed her a few tricks: I styled her hair, added a few extensions, and exchanged the glasses for contact lenses. We went shopping and bought clothes that were not only sexy, but also flattering to her body type.

She decided to try out her new look the next day at work. It was amazing that just this simple transformation gave such a boost to her self-esteem! She walked into that building with her head held high and a smile on her face. Her new look gave her confidence, which, in turn, brought on a fierce attitude that screamed, *I can be sexy because I AM sexy!* It was great to watch men do a double-take when she walked by. Not only did she get the attention of the man she secretly had a crush on, but several others as well. Think you have to be a Size 4 to be gorgeous, ladies? Think again! You ARE gorgeous … you just have to let it out!

The Woman's Survival Guide
(Because Every Woman Needs a Plan)

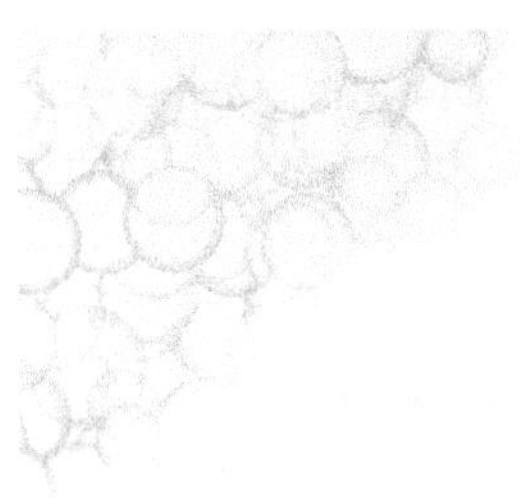

adies, we need to empower ourselves, but how? We empower ourselves when we protect ourselves. Through education, we become self-sufficient, and by being self-sufficient, we become independent. When we become independent, we place ourselves in a position to reject negative energy in our relationships. When you are dependent, there is a tendency to take whatever comes your way. There are a number of reasons we stay in unproductive, unhealthy relationships. Maybe it's for the sake of the children, because we don't feel like we can do any better, or because we feel no one else will want us. When you are independent, you can and will make better choices.

The emotional repercussions of a breakup or divorce can be extremely difficult to deal with. When a marriage or long-term relationship ends, it is usually the woman who is at a disadvantage, but by focusing on the economic, financial, and legal aspect, you can begin to reconstruct your life. No one gets married thinking it is going to end in divorce. We all want to believe in the 'happily ever after'. We say our vows truly believing and hoping it will be 'till death do us part. But let's face it: Sometimes happily ever after comes to an end, and when it does, you need a plan. Live your life as if your man can and will walk out and leave at any given moment with no warning. Think about it. If this should happen to you, would you be able to maintain the lifestyle in which you now live?

We are naturally programmed to see our mates as our mates for life, but sadly, the statistics do not match our natural inclinations. When the love is gone and the marriage and/ or relationship is over, a war can ensue. Sometimes — like it or not — you are forced to fight in order to maintain what is rightfully yours. Very seldom at the end of a marriage or relationship will a husband or partner come to his wife and offer to be fair and take care of existing and future needs. If he does, this usually means he already has someone else and just wants out. But ultimately, it is your responsibility to protect yourself financially and otherwise. By following a few simple guidelines, you can make this transition go smoothly:

✓ **ALWAYS K**EEP A **S**EPARATE **B**ANK **A**CCOUNT

Most married couples or couples in long-term relationships believe in pooling their money, so joint bank accounts are common, but every woman needs her own separate account. Even if you are a housewife, homemaker or stay-at-home mom, take a certain percentage of the household income prior to paying the household expenses and put into a savings account that only you know about; maybe into a CD, IRA, or some type of retirement plan. Consult a financial advisor in order to determine what your options are. Before you start thinking of this as a deceitful practice, think again. Men do it all the time. Some maintain bank accounts or separate credit cards that the wife knows nothing about. They may even secretly own properties. If men can do it, so can we. It's not deceitful; it's simply being smart!

✓ Learn to Meet Your Own Needs

Education is the key to independence. Not everyone has the benefit of a college degree, of course, but you should be able to develop some type of skill that will enable you to go out into the world and earn a living. Once again, homemakers and stay-at-home moms, if you have no trade or skill, take advantage of any available opportunities to further your education. Most educational facilities offer flexible schedules, but if you are not able to physically attend classes, consider taking online training courses. Maybe consider starting a business you can operate from home. Check the Internet for business ideas; the possibilities are endless. Just be sure you know how to do something that will generate some income. This issue is so important to me because my father left my mother when I was about ten years old. I have two younger brothers and a sister. My mother had no job; she had never worked outside the home a day in her life. Her job was being a stay-at-home mom taking care of her children, her husband, and her home. She had no formal education and no marketable skills, which made entering into the work force for the first time at the age of thirty practically impossible. As a result, she had to settle for whatever she could find, which was working in a sewing factory for less than minimum wage. Do not allow your man to be your only means of financial support, for through this, he can control you.

✓ **Always Maintain an Accurate Account of Your Credit File**

Know your FICO score and understand what is going on with your finances. Sometimes spouses can acquire credit cards and other financial accounts in your name without you even being aware until something like a divorce happens and you then become financially responsible for those accounts as well. It is also very important that you keep your credit in good standing. If you should happen to find yourself facing a pending divorce, you will need a good credit history to re-establish yourself.

✓ **Have Some Assets in Your Name**

Get involved in the household finances. If you are married, know what your assets are. Do not leave your financial future up to your spouse. You must realize that your man is not being noble when he claims he wants to take care of everything so you don't have to worry your pretty little head with it. Get involved! Keep backup records, and do not wait until you are faced with pending divorce to start scrambling to find hidden assets.

When you make major purchases together such as homes, real estate, automobiles, boats, RVs, etc., insist that your name is included on any deeds, leases, or titles. As a word of caution, if you are not married to a man, do not accept an automobile as a gift from him unless your name is included on the title and registration. If you do and your relationship should end, be prepared to start walking or taking public transportation. I have seen many women have their vehicles legally repossessed by an angered ex-partner, and there is absolutely nothing you can do about it. If you do accept the gift, consider it a loaner while you get yourself together.

✓ Be Cautious When Settling for Living Together or Shacking

Sandra and her fiancé Lawrence made the decision to move in together in January. They were planning to get married in September, so the move was financially beneficial for both of them because it allowed them to eliminate unnecessary extra living expenses. This agreement allowed them to put money away for their impending wedding ceremony.

Sandra had three teenage sons: eleven, thirteen, and eighteen. Lawrence had one son, a twelve-year-old. Immediately, Sandra and Lawrence began to disagree on how their sons were being raised. Lawrence felt Sandra was giving her boys too much responsibility. Her eleven- and thirteen-year-olds were allowed to cook simple dishes for themselves and would often stay at home unsupervised after school.

Sandra felt Lawrence was spoiling his twelve-year-old son and still treated him like a baby. He even picked out the clothes the boy was to wear each day. Three months after the move, they had an argument so severe that they decided to end the relationship. Since the lease on the house was in Sandra's name, Lawrence and his son had to move out, but when Sandra returned home later that evening, she discovered that her electricity had been shut off. Without much forethought, they had put the electrical service in Lawrence's name only. Ladies, when we are in love, it is hard to see a man's less desirable qualities, but just because we may not see them doesn't mean they don't exist. Chances are, when you break up with a man, he will be angry and try to hurt you or get revenge in some way. If that means disconnecting any existing services that may be in his name, most men will do it. He knows it will cause a nasty inconvenience for you. If you want to avoid finding yourself with no electricity or gas in the middle of February, take the necessary precautions to protect yourself:

1. If your live-in relationship ends and you are the party who remains in the home, you have the responsibility of taking care of yourself, and time is of the essence. Have the locks changed if you can, and if any utility services remain in your ex's name, immediately have the services transferred or reopened in your name only.

2. Never agree to get a place together unless your name is included on everything: the lease or deed and all the utilities. If he won't agree to

> this, maybe he isn't the one you should be moving in with.
> 3. Never — under ANY circumstances — move into a man's home that he already owns or leases unless you have a backup plan.

✓ Keep in Contact with Friends and Family

In the past, I have foolishly discontinued close platonic friendships because the man I was with felt threatened by my relationship with my male friends. An insecure man will always try to deter you from having friends, particularly those of the opposite sex. However, it is important to keep the channels of communication open with your friends and family. If your relationship with your man ends, the friend you eliminated from your circle could have possibly been the friend who would have provided support when you are going through difficult times. Don't give up your friendships for a man, and if he expects you to, that should be a warning sign. If he truly loves you, he will understand that your friendships are important to you, and he will not want to cut you off from other people who make you happy.

✓ Do Your Homework When Seeking Legal Counsel

Be sure that whomever you choose to represent you, whether in a divorce case, a custody hearing, or any legal capacity, is someone you feel is looking out for your best interest. Don't think just because you retain the services of an attorney that they will automatically look out for you. In many cases, women come out of a divorce with far less than they are entitled to just because the attorney wants to get their case settled as quickly as possible, or maybe he is friends with the opposing attorney. When you hire someone and pay them, you need to make sure they are doing their job. Don't be afraid to ask questions about anything you don't understand.

If you don't feel an attorney has your best interest at heart, find one who does.

✓ BEWARE OF THE MAN WITH THE 'DON'T HAVE SYNDROME'

Nothing brings a woman down faster than a man with the 'Don't Have Syndrome' — you know, the guy who doesn't have a car, doesn't have his own place (living in his mama's basement doesn't count), and especially one who doesn't have a JOB! If a man cannot provide for himself and you allow him to move into your home, you're setting yourself up for trouble in the future.

✓ QUESTION EVERYTHING YOU DO NOT UNDERSTAND

If you meet a man and he doesn't have a car, why not? If he does not have his own place, what is the reason? If he is evasive about his past, what is he hiding? Learn to recognize warning signs. For example, if a man has never had a place of his own and he moved straight from his mama's house into his baby mama's house to your house, he may have a problem accepting responsibility.

✓ RECOGNIZING IRRESPONSIBILITY

Now I know this probably sounds unbelievable, but you would be surprised at how many women can't recognize irresponsibility. Before you commit yourself to a relationship you should learn a man's true character, and this is something that won't happen overnight, but over time. You determine a man's character not just by listening to what he tells you, but by also observing his actions. How many times have you gotten involved in a relationship and later wished you hadn't? This is why it is important to observe a man before committing yourself to a long-term relationship. You observe him to determine not only his integrity, but also his level of responsibility. Watch how he pays his bills, and if he has children does he uphold his financial responsibility? If you have been dating for a substantial amount of time, oh say a year, and his lights, water and phone have been turned off during that period, it shows a lack of responsibility. If he doesn't have his own place and he is driving around in a car with 26' rims that are valued more than the car is worth *and* they are *RENTED*, he is irresponsible! Who really wants to deal with this drama? And if you are involved with a man who lives his life by these standards there will eventually be drama. A man who displays irresponsible behavior during a relationship doesn't usually transform into Mr. Responsible in marriage, so before you say "I do" you need to know his character.

Most women — myself included — fall into the category of being nurturers. We often *want* to help a man get on his feet. I agree that sometimes, a man may be going through some difficult times, perhaps by no fault of his own. With the economy as it is, everyone is capable of having some downfalls, and most women take it upon themselves to help him get back on his feet. After all, isn't that what a good woman is supposed to do? We tell ourselves that if we stick by him through the bad times, when he finally gets himself together, we will reap the benefit and enjoy the good times. But it is all too common for women to work to put their men through school, and as soon as he gets that degree and great job, his lady is no longer good enough or young enough for him. Or maybe you allow him to use your automobile. Are you sure he isn't putting mileage on your car and using your gas to go visit and/or take another woman out? If you've allowed him to crash in your home, is he using it to entertain other women while you're out working? This might sound farfetched, and you might think, *my man would never do that*, but these scandalous events are happening to women every day. Don't be afraid to ask questions because you deserve to know the answers.

✓ **DOCUMENT EVERYTHING**

Keep written records, receipts, notes, anything that you may possibly have to use at a later date. There is nothing worse than trying to prove your case when you have no proof. We want to trust the man we choose to be in a relationship with, but sometimes we can be so trusting that it clouds our better judgment. If you have evidence that your man has been unfaithful, be able to provide documentation. If your man has been physically abusive, it is your responsibility to prove that it actually happened. We are living in the age of technology, which makes it simple to document any situation. There are many tools available to assist you in monitoring and tracking. Your local electronics store is a great source when looking for tools to assist you as well. Invest in a mini voice-activated tape recorder and a telephone recording device that allows you to tape both sides of all telephone activity. (It is illegal in some states to record a person's conversation without their knowledge, so be sure to check the laws in your local area before recording any telephone conversations.) If you have suspicions, it is better to be prepared, for you never know when you may have to take the stand in court, and your best witness is always written or documented proof.

Lisa, a twenty-nine-year-old pharmacist, met her husband of five years in high school. She told me of an incident that occurred during their first year of marriage. They were having extreme financial problems. With a mortgage, credit card bills, and student loan debts piling up, they were living as most people are: paycheck to paycheck. Then, to make matters worse, Lisa's husband lost his job. During one of their heated money discussions, Lisa turned to walk away from her husband. He was upset because she turned her back on him, so he shoved her from behind. In the process, her shoe caught on the coffee table, and she fell, hitting her head on the bookcase. As a result, she ended up with a black eye.

Of course, he was apologetic and said he would never again touch her in anger, so Lisa let it go. After all, it was an accident. She loved her husband and knew he would never intentionally hurt her, but she did have enough sense to photograph her injuries. True to his word, for three years, he never touched her in anger — until he lost his job once again and became depressed after not immediately finding work. One night after work, Lisa decided to go to happy hour with the girls to have a few drinks. When she returned home, her husband was angry because she chose to go out with her girlfriends rather than come home to him. They argued, and words were exchanged. Lisa's husband grabbed her around the neck and shoved her into the wall, continuing to put pressure on her throat. After a struggle, he suddenly let her fall to the floor. Lisa decided it was time to end the marriage and filed for divorce, using physical abuse as one of the grounds. Her husband denied the allegation of abuse, but Lisa was able to prove her case based on the pictures from the previous incident, even though her husband had no prior history of violence.

✓ DO NOT Participate in Excuses

Benjamin Franklin once said, "He that is good for making excuses is seldom good for anything else," and this is so true. It is not your job to protect your man's reputation. Do not make excuses for any of your man's unacceptable behavior — big or small — and do not accept excuses when he isn't treating you or your relationship properly. For instance, there is absolutely no excuse for a man being unemployed. Any healthy, able-bodied, mature, *responsible* man will have a job or be fervently looking for one (and I mean REALLY looking for one every day until he finds one). If you find yourself constantly having to rationalize, validate and justify your man's shortcomings, you are participating in excuses. Don't be your man's excuse to fail!

We must learn that we do not need a man to validate who we are and we should set some standards for the man we want in our life so that we can save ourselves from disappointment later. Don't get involved with a man simply because he wants you. You do not have to settle. Be selective and choose a partner who has something to contribute to the relationship other than sex. I have heard African American women say there is a shortage of 'good Black men'. "They are either in jail, on drugs, gay, or with White women." This is totally untrue, ladies. Speaking as a Black woman, there is no shortage of men, Black, White, or other. The problem seems to be that some of you are not presenting yourself in a favorable manner in which to attract these good men. Go where the men are! By this, I don't necessarily mean go to the clubs or bars, but it is possible to meet men where they hang out. The gym, sporting events, and even the car wash are excellent places to meet men. I have met men in the supermarket, at service stations, and even at the traffic light. As the old adage goes, "Sometimes you have to kiss some toads in order to find your prince." We simply must change our way of thinking. When you program your mind to believe that there are no good men out there it makes you desperate, and women often make bad decisions out of desperation. This way of thinking can make a woman latch on to any man that shows her a little attention because in her mind, something is better than nothing.

To overcome this way of thinking, an excellent idea is to make a list of what you require in a man and a relationship. Use your list as a guide for selecting your potential mate, but be realistic with your expectations. In my younger years, my basic requirements list went something like this:

1. He must be gainfully employed (earning more than minimum wage).
2. He must have his own place.
3. He must have a car. It doesn't have to be a Benz, but he must have a working vehicle.
4. He must have some goals in life.
5. He must have okay credit.
6. He must not have more than two baby mamas.
7. He must have a strong belief in God.
8. He must love his mother and respect all women, children, and living creatures.

Having preset expectations and not implementing them defeats the purpose. I learned from my mistakes because sometimes, against my better judgment, I would disregard my list when getting involved with a man. Out of my eight requirements, he may have only met three, yet I would still get involved with him. Had I stuck with my basic requirements, there were some situations I would have never allowed myself to get involved in. The older and wiser I got, the more my basic requirements were upgraded. I look at life differently now than I did when I was younger, so these days, my requirements would go something like this:

1. He must be financially secure (but I'm flexible). Not only must he be employed, but he must also bring to the table at least what I earn or better.
2. He must have his own place.
3. He must have a working vehicle.
4. He must have achieved some goals in life and be continually striving to improve his (and our) quality of life.
5. He should have a better-than-average credit score (but I'm flexible).
6. He must not have more than one baby mama.
7. He must have a strong belief in God and put God first in his life.
8. He must love his mother and respect all women, children, and living creatures.

At this point in my life, I realize that if I follow God's plan, the man I choose to have in my life would be all of the things I mentioned above and then some. This is the plan that I will adhere to for the rest of my life:

**I want a man to take on the roles
and responsibilities of a MAN!
That means one that does what God
called man to do.**

* Govern his household and be the *head* of his household
* Supports himself *and* his household
* To put his wife as his highest Earthly loyalty; to honor her, provide for her physical, emotional, financial, sexual, intellectual and spiritual needs
* To provide for, love, teach and discipline his children
* To be the spiritual leader in the home

This book is not and was never intended to be about male bashing, it wasn't written to point out everything that men do wrong, but it is a realistic look at relationships through the eyes of women — ordinary, everyday women. Having been married five times, it should be obvious that I love men, and I do not intend to imply that men are the only ones who cheat, lie, deceive, and betray. Some women cheat as often as men and are known to be better at it than men.

I also know there are some strong, loving men out there who would never cheat. I have had the pleasure of knowing and loving a few of them. But faithfulness alone does not make a successful relationship. In the past, after choosing to leave a relationship an ex said to me, "I did everything I could! I didn't cheat and I brought my paycheck home." Ladies is having your financial needs met really enough?! Well it wasn't enough for me and I'm hoping that some of my male readers will be able to relate to the stories and issues contained in this book. Guys, the chapters *What Every Man Should Know about Women* and *Romantic Things Women Love* were written just for you. In reading this book, I hope you gain understanding by seeing what women think and feel ... and why we feel as we do. But primarily, this book was written to give hope and healing to women.

Oh the Drama!

et's talk drama. Drama is as natural as breathing. It is quite natural to feel hurt and anger when we open ourselves up to our loved ones and they betray us. If you watch popular reality shows like *Cheaters,* you'll see that emotions are warranted. If you suspect your man of cheating, know that first of all, there is nothing you can do to stop it. Following him and checking up on his voicemails, cell phone calls, texts, and emails are not going to make him stop. In fact, this type of behavior only makes him better at covering his tracks. However, you can take control of your life, even when you feel your relationship is coming apart at the seams. Don't allow your suspicions or investigations to throw you out of control. If you feel you have reason to believe something shady is going on, then it probably is. Women normally won't be suspicious without cause, and if the evidence is there, you need to be strong enough to either work through it or end it.

Tracy, a thirty-five-year-old from Korea, shared her story of infidelity. A few years ago, her husband of twelve years began taking vacations to Paris—alone. Tracy never thought anything strange about this because she knew her husband's college frat brother, who was also best man at their wedding, lived in Paris.

Every couple of years was designated as reunion time for the guys — a time for them to relax, catch up on old times, and get away from their jobs, women, and children for a while. Boys just wanna have fun too, right?

After one of his return trips, Tracy noticed her husband was buying lots of international calling cards. This eventually led her to notice he was spending a lot more time on the phone. Normally, this wouldn't have been so suspicious, but whenever she walked into the room, he would abruptly end his phone call. When he wasn't on the phone, he was locked away in their guest bedroom on the computer for long periods of time.

After observing his suspicious behavior for a while, Tracy got wise and connected a telephone recording device to their home telephone. She found that her husband was communicating with a lady he had met while vacationing in Paris. She listened in horror and anger as they discussed how much they enjoyed the time they had spent together. She learned from listening in on these conversations that this affair had been going on for at least two years. She also heard her husband and his mistress discussing building a future together. Tracy gathered all the evidence and confronted her husband. He initially denied the affair — even as she produced the tapes.

Through the process of investigating her husband's deceit, Tracy discovered the mistress's phone number. Of course, the mistress was more than happy to fill Tracy in on all the details of her relationship with her husband and how it came about; the other woman often likes to brag about her conquests. The mistress had always known that Tracy's husband, her lover, was a married man. After several phone conversations with the mistress, Tracy's way of handling this situation was to invite her husband's mistress to the States for a visit and allow her to stay in her home so she could get the full understanding of what was really going on. Her husband reluctantly agreed to this visit, but he made it clear that this was Tracy's guest, and he wanted no part in it. Tracy even went so far as to pick her husband's mistress up from the airport when she arrived.

She allowed her husband's mistress to stay in her home for a week. During this week, they did everything together: grocery shopping, picking the kids up from school, and even household chores, but mostly they talked. Tracy wanted to include the mistress in their daily activities so she could see that she was really breaking up a home and family. But the mistress's motive for the visit was to try and persuade Tracy's husband to return with her to Paris. The affair was clearly out in the open, but Tracy's husband was not willing to give up his home and family, so he ended the affair. Tracy stayed with her husband and forgave his affair, she said, for the sake of the children.

Now, I definitely would never, under any circumstance, invite my husband's mistress into my home. When I asked Tracy the same question most of you would ask, "What were you thinking?" her answer was, "I wanted to know what was going on. My husband was denying the affair, and his mistress was admitting it. I wanted to get the two together and see whose story would change. At the same time, I wanted to be able to keep my eye on her at all times, and where better to do that than in my own home?" I still didn't get it, but I guess women from different cultures react differently in certain situations.

If there is an indiscretion in your marriage or long-term partnership, it will be up to you to decide if that relationship is worth saving. Tracy decided to forgive — but I doubt she, her husband, or even the mistress will ever truly forget.

Many years ago, I was taught a lesson by a man I considered a professional cheater, and because I won't mention his name, we'll call him 'Chuck'. I thought Chuck was the total package: mid-thirties, reasonably attractive, CEO of a major corporation, driving a power car, living in a typical bachelor pad, and a former NFL player to boot. He was doing his thing, and I was impressed. I was even more impressed when he started taking me out. He treated me to nothing but the best, and there were dinners, theaters, and shopping trips. But one thing I noticed was that we always went out of town; we never went anywhere locally. When I asked him why, he answered, "Oh, this town is not good enough for my lady. I want to take you somewhere special because you deserve it." Of course, that shut me up for a minute, so I would sit back and enjoy the ride.

Eventually, all the traveling got old. I was tired of going ninety miles just to catch dinner and a movie. I began to suspect that Chuck may be married, and I began to ask questions. He always maintained that he was a single man with no wife and no other women. After a few weeks, I gave Chuck an ultimatum: "If the only way we can be together is to leave town, then we might as well end our relationship."

He adamantly refused to end it, so, needless to say, we started hanging out in our hometown. I was elated. *I got my way, so he must truly love me,* I thought. Soon, though, I started noticing that when we did go to a movie, he spent more time watching the entrance than the movie. He was always jumpy and jittery. Soon afterwards, I began putting the facts together.

While on the phone with Chuck one night about three months into our relationship, I heard a woman's voice in the background. After what sounded like a struggle, the line went dead. I hit redial, only to get a busy signal. It was late, and I was already in bed, but I came up with the brilliant idea of getting dressed and driving over to his townhouse to find out what the hell was going on. When I arrived, got out of my vehicle, and started up the sidewalk, I passed a woman carrying a cardboard box. It was dark, and I couldn't see her face clearly, but I could tell she was crying. I had the feeling she had just come out of Chuck's apartment. The front door was open, and Chuck was sitting on the sofa casually drinking a beer. He didn't seem at all surprised to see me. Naturally, I asked who the woman was and why she was there. Chuck said she was just someone who he had broken it off with three months prior, right before we started dating. He claimed she had left some things at his apartment, and unknowingly to him, she had also kept a key that she used to enter his place without his permission. I asked why he didn't call the police, and he claimed, "She was pretty messed up, and she's just having a hard time accepting that it is truly over." While wrapping me in a tight embrace and nibbling my neck, Chuck assured me that everything was taken care of and that she was now completely out of his life. He was so attentive and loving that I couldn't help but let it slide.

Not long afterwards, I began to notice that whenever we went out, this particular woman was always somewhere around. If we left the movies, she would just happen to be driving by as we were backing out of the parking lot. If we went out to dinner and came out of the restaurant, she would be leaning up against her car in the parking lot. She never said anything, but I could tell she wanted to make sure we saw her. I never put two and two together and realized that this was the same woman I had seen leaving his apartment crying weeks prior — at least not until another incident occurred.

The air conditioning unit in Chuck's apartment went out. He called to say he would be staying in a hotel for a few days until the maintenance crew was able to replace his unit. On this same day, we had a date to go to a go-cart racetrack. I met Chuck at his apartment, and from there, we took his BMW to the racetrack. Upon pulling into the parking lot at the fun park, this now very familiar Toyota Camry pulled in behind us. In the visor mirror, I could see it was the same woman that had been shadowing us for the last few weeks. She continued to sit in her car, and I could see Chuck watching her through the rearview mirror as he asked, "Are you ready to go?"

I exploded and demanded to know what the hell was going on and who the woman was who was following us. "And don't try to tell me again that you don't know and that this is another coincidence. I've seen this girl following us too many times!" I said angrily.

Chuck excused himself and said, "You sit tight and let me handle this. I'll only be a minute."

I sat in the car and watched as he approached her driver's side window. He proceeded to calmly have a conversation with the woman. She began to cry, took what appeared to be a ring off her finger, and threw it at him before she recklessly drove off.

Meanwhile, I began to do a slow burn. When Chuck returned to the car, I told him I was tired of his lies and of allowing him to make a fool of me. "Don't say anything. Take me back to my car, and I never want to see your lying ass again." I quickly shut down any conversation on the trip back to my car; I didn't want to hear anything he had to say. When we reached his apartment complex, I got into my car and left.

Later that day, Chuck called from the hotel to apologize and to say that it was truly over with his ex. "She finally got the message, and she knows I'm with you now." he said. "She will not be a problem for us anymore."

I felt my reserve start to weaken as I accepted his apology, but then, I heard a knock on his hotel room door. I also heard a female voice say, "Chuck, open this door!" My anger level shot through the roof once again, as the line went dead. I went into my closet, got my 380 semi-automatic pistol, dropped it into my purse, got into my Mustang GT, and drove over to his hotel.

When I knocked on his room door, he opened it. I went in and looked around. I checked the bathroom and the closet while he sat watching me from the bed, but there was no one else in the room. I pulled my 380 from my purse and suggested he start explaining. He was frozen in fear. The look of horror on his face made me feel so powerful; for once I had the upper hand. He started stuttering as he tried to explain. He told me her name was Yvonne and that he had dated her briefly before meeting me. She was a nurse and also a junkie, strung out on prescription pain pills. When he broke it off with her three months earlier, she didn't want to accept that the relationship was over, so every time we went out, she made a habit of following us. He said he had hoped with time that she would get over it and stop stalking him.

I asked him how she knew he was staying at the hotel, and he said, "She must have followed us from the fun park." After hearing his words once again, 'The only lady I want in my life is you ...'" I let my guard down and put my gun away.

Not two seconds later, there was another knock on the door. A voice said, "Chuck, this is Rita. Open this door!"

I was confused. "Rita?! I thought you said her name was Yvonne?"

He said nothing.

"Chuck, either you open that door or I will!"

He continued to sit on the bed, dumbfounded, just shaking his head.

I opened the door. Immediately, the bitch I now knew as Rita raised her hand, and the next thing I knew, we were going at it. Also, let me say that my part in this was not about a man, but no one raises their hand to strike me without consequences.

After Chuck managed to separate us, she sat down and began to explain her side of the story to me. Rita told me she had been dating Chuck off and on for seven years — seven years! He moved her from her home in Los Angeles (where he was playing with the NFL) to our hometown seven years prior. During those seven years, he had continued to cheat on her. She also said they were still together as a couple during the past few months while he was seeing me. She said, "We had coordinated time schedules. When he leaves you early, he spends those nights with me. On the days he leaves me early, he will spend the night with you. Girl, he is good. He tells us exactly what we want to hear. Chuck has a rule that no one spends the night at his place. That way, if you or I look for him, he can always tell us he was called in to work."

I knew Rita was telling the truth because she had nothing to lose but a fool-hearted cheater boyfriend. I had questioned Chuck on many occasions as to why he would spend some nights at my place, but I was never allowed to stay with him. I surmised that it was because he was always on call. His work schedule worked to his advantage because it made it convenient for Chuck to play us both.

Rita continued by saying that she had caught Chuck with three other women the week before.

I was baffled, but when I regained my composure, I asked her, "If you know that he is cheating on you with all these other women, why would you continue to be with him?"

She started crying and said, "Because I love him! I love him, and I don't know what else to do."

She loves him? I thought. *She must be ill*! I replied, "Well, I feel sorry for you and I *do* know what to do! From this point on, I don't want to see his lying, no fucking, tired ass again," I said.

Rita laughed through her tears. "You are so right. He has a real problem getting an erection, but I assume it is because he is sleeping with so many of us."

Chuck, still sitting on the bed, shook his head and said, "I can't help it. I ain't no good."

I wanted to smack him upside his head with my 380, which was still in my purse. Instead, I checked my appearance in the mirror, re-applied my lipstick, and like the lady I am, I left. He wasn't worth it.

I felt it important to address this issue because it could have easily gone in another direction. I was so angry when I went into that room. I was tired of being made to feel like a fool. I wouldn't listen when another male friend tried to warn me that Chuck was cheating. I even accused my friends of lying to me about Chuck, claiming they were just jealous. I never knew they were warning me because they didn't want to see me hurt. I was so angry that I went into that room with the intention of using my gun — not to hurt him necessarily, but to scare the living, cheating hell out of him. I'll admit, the look on Chuck's face as he stared down the barrel of my weapon gave me such a rush. I felt like, *Yeah, I can do this.* With my anger as it was, the situation could have easily gotten out of control. Someone could have gotten hurt — maybe even killed — and my life as I know it could have been over. I could have been locked up for life, for what? A no-good, lying man! I thank God for being with me that day and for keeping me under control. This is an example of how drama can get totally out of hand. There are so many women locked away in prison today because their anger got the best of them. Ladies, remember that a cheating man isn't worth a smudge of your mascara, let alone a life sentence.

Within fifteen minutes of returning to my apartment, Chuck arrived. He was beating on my door apologizing and pleading with me to let him explain. I quickly informed him that if he did not leave, I would call the police.

Was I hurt? Yes. I was completely humiliated. I was sick and sobbing. I had fallen in love with this man who hurt me so badly. But what did I do?

First, I changed my phone number. Ladies, you will be surprised at how well this works to your advantage. When we break up with a man and decide not to talk to him, we screen our calls. We don't want to talk to him, but we do want to know that he's calling. When you change your phone number, you eliminate that added stress. It will keep you from waiting on his calls because you know he has no way of reaching you. It also keeps you from being weak should his call happen to slip through. This kind of 'cold turkey' cut off will help you heal.

Then, I went shopping, and the very next day while walking through the mall, guess who I came across walking hand in hand? You got it! Chuck and Rita! I looked at her, shook my head, and continued my sexy stroll.

A few seconds later, she caught up to me, smiling, and said, "Girl, I wish I was strong like you, but I gotta give him another chance."

I looked her in the eye and said with all honesty, "Good luck," and I knew she would need it.

As strong as she said I was, this incident was not easy for me. If by chance I saw Chuck out in public, I refused to acknowledge his presence. I got through this by having a firm resolve, a strong backbone, and prayer.

Needy, insecure women are unattractive. While Rita continued to be needy, Chuck showed no respect. He knew that whatever he did, she would continue to be there. On the other hand, when I cut all ties with Chuck, he is still, to this day, attracted to what he can't have.

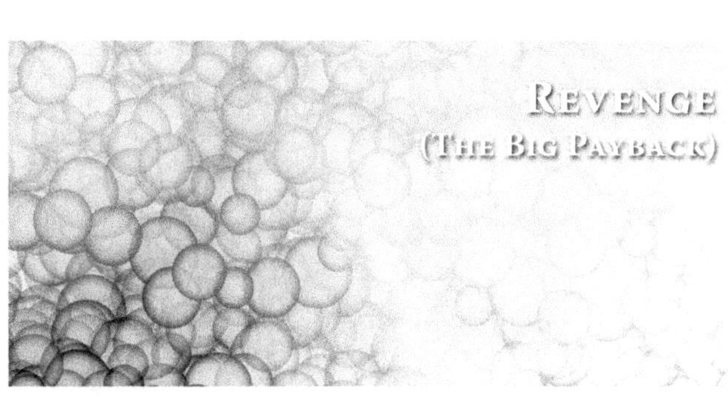

REVENGE
(THE BIG PAYBACK)

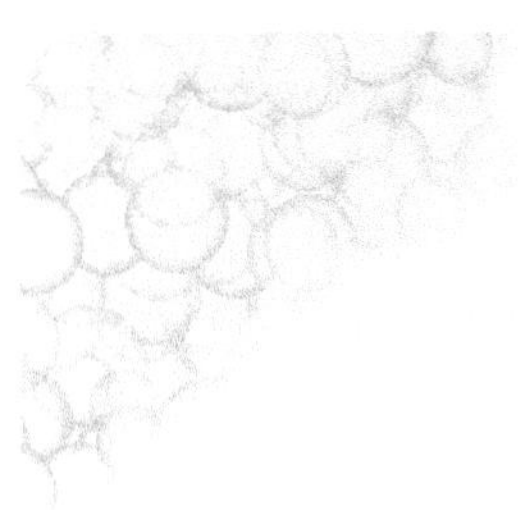

The ultimate betrayal is infidelity. Being jilted by a lover can make you want to crawl under a rock and die. Some women experience extreme depression and withdraw from the outside world. Some become so withdrawn they can't eat or sleep. For some women, though, it is just the opposite; they turn to food for comfort and overeat. Some may retreat to their beds and hibernate there, not emerging for weeks. When a man cheats on you, your self-esteem will be at an all-time low, but after agonizing over what has happened and reflecting on your newly single status, there will come a point when grief and sadness will give way to overwhelming rage.

During this time, we can spend hours, days or even weeks, plotting and planning our ex's downfall. Some women will do just about anything to get back at him. While some women settle for the personal satisfaction of throwing a brick through the windshield of his brand new Range Rover as it's parked outside his new woman's house at two a.m., others will take it a step further and report him to the IRS for tax evasion. Revenge may be a 'dish best served cold', but it comes in a variety of flavors.

Jessica had been with her man for six years. When she met him, he was in a committed relationship with his baby's mama, who was also his live-in girlfriend. For six years, Jessica had been content to be the other woman, but recently, her man had been displaying what she considered suspicious behavior. He began not returning phone calls, breaking dates, and not spending the time he usually spent with her.

Jessica was tireless in her pursuit of revenge, completely consumed by her quest for payback. She took days off work and drove hours to stake out her ex's new woman's home. During one of Jessica's snoop escapades (opening his mail), she discovered her man had recently purchased a vehicle that she had never seen him drive. Now, she faced a confusing dilemma. *Who in the hell is driving that car?* She wondered.

Jessica knew her man was known for buying vehicles for his women. He had previously bought one for his current live-in girlfriend, and also during their relationship, he had purchased a vehicle for her. So now, Jessica was on a fact-finding mission. She had the year, make, and model of this phantom vehicle, but she had to find out who was driving it. By going online and creating an account through his wireless provider, she began checking his phone records. Wouldn't you know it? There was one number that showed up consistently. By going online and doing a reverse search, she tracked the woman's name and address. Hence, the stakeouts began, and last I heard, Jessica was still there.

Revenge, although it seems like a good idea at the time, takes up too much of the time and energy we should be devoting to taking care of ourselves and moving on. In order to recover, it is necessary to release the hurt and anger caused by a betrayal, but at some point, you have to learn how to get over it. If a man decides he doesn't want to be with you any longer, have some dignity. Know that you shouldn't want to be with someone who doesn't want to be with you. Acting like an alley cat only makes him realize he made the right decision by leaving you alone.

Take Jessica, for instance. Her life was consumed with investigating what she already knew to be true: If a man cheats *with* you, he will cheat *on* you. Until you let go of obsessive behavior, you can never move forward in life. When you allow yourself to get over it, move on without him, and become a better person because of what you learned from your mistake, you will then have true and fulfilling revenge. The greatest revenge is successfully living without him!

How to Get the Man You Want to Marry You

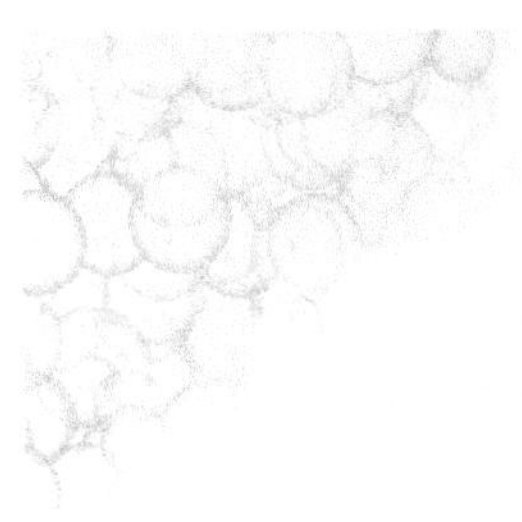

I get very different reactions from men and women when I tell them I have been married five times. Most men are intrigued; they want to know what it is about me that made five men want to make me their wife. Women are curious; they want to know what I did and how I did it in order to get five men to make a commitment to marriage. Women often ask, "I can't get one man to marry me, and you've had five! Is there something wrong with me? Is there something I'm not doing right?"

Just because you are not married and have never been proposed to does not mean there is something wrong with you. You may not be aware of what men are looking for when selecting a wife. Half the time, men don't know what they are looking for in a wife until it is staring them in the face. The key to getting a man to want to make you his wife is quite simple. Notice I said, get *him* to want to marry *you* — and that means without you ever bringing up the subject, dropping hints, or leaving wedding planner guides on the coffee table. The key is that you must *be* the woman he wants to marry. How? You do this by simply working on you. You have to be the person you wish to find. When you have yourself together, men will come at you from every direction. This does not mean you have to change who you are, but if what you're doing is not working, it's time to try something different. In order for a man to see all of your good qualities, you have to possess self-confidence and see the good in you as well. You must feel that you are worthy of having goodness in your life. As we've already discussed, men are attracted to confident, sexy women, and when you love yourself, it shows in everything that you do.

✓ ALWAYS BE WELL GROOMED

Your hair should always be clean and in good condition, and your nails should be neat and trimmed. Pay special attention to problem areas like your heels, toenails, knees, and elbows, and make it part of your regular routine maintenance to have a monthly scheduled manicure and pedicure. Shave or wax body hair. You should always look your best. All women have those days when you may be around the house cleaning or out working in the yard and you think of something you need to run out and pick up from the store. You think to yourself, *I really should clean up a little, comb my hair, maybe put on a little lipstick, but naah ... I'm only running to the corner store. No one will even see me.* But what if someone DOES see you? What if that day, at that very corner store, an absolutely gorgeous man is stopping in to buy a soda? It happens to me every time, without fail. This can also be a good thing, in some cases, as if you meet a man when you feel you are not looking your best and he is still interested, he could be worth getting to know. After all, he is seeing the real you — not the perfectly dressed, made-up you. However, it is always best to get into the habit of looking your best when you go out, so take a little extra effort with your appearance. Good personal hygiene is extremely important, so always be clean and fresh. Even men who are slobs themselves notice everything when it pertains to their lady.

✓ THINK SEXY ... BE SEXY!

Always make a habit of wearing sexy underwear! Matching bras and panties are a must. Why? Because it will help you think and feel sexy ... and that will help you be sexy! Ladies, it is time to do some spring cleaning. Throw away all those old, worn-out underwear. You know the ones I'm talking about — the ones you hold on to because you think they are so comfortable. There is nothing sexy about faded fabric and elastic so dry rotted it is falling apart. Get rid of it! You don't want your man seeing those — not even by accident.

Maintain your sexuality even when preparing for bed. The most common response from women is that when they go to bed, they want to be comfortable. That's fine, but you need to recognize that it is possible to be sexy and comfortable at the same time. I'm not suggesting you wear a tight-laced bustier, stocking, garters, and heels, but there is such a variety of sexy sleepwear available on the market today. There is no excuse for not being sexy and comfortable at the same time. For example, try a basic, simple silk nightie or a pair of cute lacy boy shorts with matching camisole. Women look incredibly sexy in high heels (especially stilettos); they complement the feet and whatever you may or may not be wearing—and most importantly, men love them! When you make these simple things a way of life, it becomes a habit. You won't think of it as getting yourself together because it becomes second nature. I firmly believe that hair rollers were not meant to be worn to bed, and yes, there are still some of you ladies out there doing it.

I remember the day my sister tried a new look with my hair. I admit it was cute, sexy, and different from my usual style. When I was preparing for bed, she took my hair and wrapped it around my head. She then put about four or five rollers in the top and tied a silk scarf around the entire do. I looked like a giant Q-tip, and it was so uncomfortable to sleep on. The next morning, I swore never to try this again. It was too much work.

A few days later, my sister asked if I was keeping up the look. I told her, "No, because I have to be cute when I go to bed," I wear my hair long and straight. When I go to bed, I pull it back into a ponytail and tie a silk scarf around it. Do you desire to look cute when you are with your man? To accomplish that, my scarf goes on my head after all other activities have taken place and only after the lights go off. When I awake in the morning, it is the first thing that comes off before I get out of bed.

Even if you don't have a man and are sleeping alone, do the extras! Just as you would get dressed to go out, get dressed for bed. Pamper yourself with a scented bubble bath, dress in a sexy teddy, and add a touch of lip color and a hint of your favorite fragrance. Don't overdo it, though; after all, you are going to bed. These simple touches are guaranteed to get your man's attention.

For years, I have been interviewing men, looking to find what is really important to them in a relationship. The most popular response was "Good sex." The complaints range from women not knowing or willing to perform oral sex to their satisfaction to not getting enough sex. Some even complained that their women had let themselves go and were simply not sexy enough.

When I asked most married men or men who were in a long-term committed relationship what their women wore to bed, the highest percentage said (and not very happily) "Shorts and a t-shirt." Ladies, I know shorts and t-shirts are comfortable, but have you really looked at yourself lately, or do you just jump into bed? I suggest the next time you get dressed for bed, take a long, hard look in the mirror. What you see is probably a lot less appealing to your man.

We already know men live for fantasy, which is why strip clubs and the porn industry are so popular. Women need to incorporate a little bit of fantasy into their everyday lives. When you give your man that fantasy, he will enjoy coming home to you. Don't make your man feel as if he has to hide his porn collection or his erotic desires from you. Men love women they can be themselves around. Show him you are open-minded. If you really want to spice up your sex life, suggest selecting and watching adult movies together. Your man will love you for it. You have the ability to make your man feel like superman. If you can make your man feel like *the* man, he's probably not going anywhere. Men who are totally fulfilled are less likely to cheat.

Part of thinking sexy is to keep in mind the things that will turn your man on. When you're getting to know him, make your home a peaceful, calming and comforting environment. Make it a place where he will look forward to coming — somewhere he will always want to be because he can relax and unwind there. Keep those special things that he enjoys on hand; his favorite drinks and music, also keep the refrigerator stocked with all the foods he loves. Don't forget the beer!

✓   **What About the Kids?**

One factor that initially attracts men to me is the fact that I don't have any children. If you have children, though, don't let this discourage you. There are ways of getting the man you want to marry you, even if you do have kids. Be open, honest, and straightforward. Let a man know upfront that you have children. It is also okay to introduce your children to your man at any point during a new relationship. However, if you feel your man may be a little hesitant because of this, let him get to know you and want you first before you start bringing him in and around your children. Once he has fallen in love with you, he won't care. This does not mean you should bring your man into your home, around your children to have sex and or spend the night. That is a no-no! First of all, most men will not respect you if you allow him to do this, and it is never a good idea to allow overnight sexual partners in your home while your children are present unless you are in a long-term, committed relationship. So, always be upfront and honest.

A male friend, Steven, once told me that while interviewing a young lady for a job, he was highly impressed with her. She was the most beautiful young woman he had ever seen. After the interview, he hired her for a position in the company, and it wasn't long before they became involved in a romantic relationship that grew so serious he asked her to move in with him. Everything was going well, and they were enjoying a great relationship. Steven enjoyed spending time with his girlfriend and her five-year-old daughter. A few months later, the company they worked for asked Steven to relocate to another branch to work out some problems within the company. This meant he would have to relocate to another city. Steven agreed to the move, as long as his girlfriend was also given a transfer so they could continue to be together. Steven's girlfriend left her young daughter in the care of her mother until they were settled into their new home. On weekends, she would return home and visit with her daughter.

One particular weekend, Steven's schedule permitted him to accompany his girlfriend home. When they arrived, six children ran out to the car to greet them yelling, "Mama's home!"

When Steven asked why all the kids were calling her 'Mama', she responded, "These are my children. My mother has legal guardianship of all of them."

Steven was shocked and overwhelmed. For the first time in their six-month relationship, he found out that she had not one, but six children. Of course, he ended the relationship, not because she had six children but because by not telling him the truth, she took away his choice as to whether or not he wanted to be with her and her six kids. So, whether you have kids or not, it is extremely important that you are honest about your circumstance.

✓ Keep a Clean House

This is extremely important. Men are comfortable in clean environments. If your home is filthy, your man may not say anything about it, but rest assured that he notices. Always look at your home through a visitor's eyes. Avoid having dirty dishes in the sink and keep your wastebaskets throughout the house emptied. In the bathroom, keep the fixtures clean, the trash dumped, and the mirrors streak-free. Keep any personal items you don't want guests to see in a separate area or storage closet, particularly feminine hygiene products and prescription medications. If you do not want your man to know you are on antidepressants, don't keep it in your medicine cabinet.

My girlfriend Tonya called me crying after her first date with Kevin. She described in detail how wonderful the date was. "After dinner he took me home," she said, "and I invited him in for a drink. We were connecting, the lights were low, and the music was grooving. Kevin was in a playful mood, and he was singing to me. Then he asked to use the bathroom. The entire time he was in the bathroom, I kept trying to remember if there was anything in there I wouldn't want him to see. Then I thought about my prescription yeast infection medication that was in the medicine cabinet. I just know he looked through my things. He was in there for an awfully long time. Then, when he came out, he made an excuse that he had to leave. His whole demeanor had changed. I am so afraid he saw something that turned him off."

Since Kevin never called her again, it is safe to say he didn't get a sudden case of diarrhea from dinner. Most likely, he did see something in her bathroom that turned him off. Tonya later realized what that something was; there was an empty condom wrapper in her wastebasket. She had learned her lesson, and now my girlfriends make sure they follow the rules. Your bathroom should be the one room in your home that is always up to standards. Your guests could ask to use it at anytime, and because it is such a personal room, they can learn a lot about you just by checking out what is in there. Since your guests are behind locked doors, they have time to go through everything. Ladies, when we visit a man's home, you know what we do. We check the trash, medicine cabinet, and bathtub drain for strands of hair. I have even gone so far as to check the condition of a man's toothbrush. If his toothbrush is not well kept and it is all grimy and worn out, it sends the message that he will put anything in his mouth — and that might be a mouth you don't want to be kissing.

✓ It's All About EGO!

Men have huge egos, right? So stroke it! When he talks, listen and really be genuinely interested in what he has to say. Men love women who pay attention, make eye contact, smile, and laugh at their jokes. Show him you are interested by giving him your undivided attention. The small gestures make a difference. Men love when you buy some small token of love and appreciation. Offer to pay for something on a date. If he treats you to dinner, offer to pay for after-dinner cocktails. More often than not, if he is a gentleman, he will refuse the offer, but the thought will truly count!

Be your man's own personal cheerleader, for as I said, it's all about ego. Ladies, you have the power to make your man feel like Superman. I was impressed that at age twenty-one, Amanda was already practicing the rules with her boyfriend Bryan. After Hurricane Katrina, the casino industry suffered a massive loss. As a result, the casino where I was employed closed for renovation for one year, so I temporarily took a job with a local cellular phone company. Our phones were provisioned with two-way radios, and my former coworker, Amanda, would frequently two-way her boyfriend during the day. She never failed to let Bryan be Superman!

One day, I witnessed a call between the two of them that went something like this:

"Hi sweetie, I'm having a really bad day," Amanda said with a pout. "I just broke my shoe, and I need you to fix it."

"Okay, baby doll. Don't worry. I'll take care of it when we get home." Bryan replied.

Amanda answered with loving admiration in her voice, "Thanks, sweetie. I knew you could do it. You can do anything!"

Amanda told me that although she knew she could take care of herself, she wanted to make Bryan feel wanted and needed. Whether it was mending a hole in her sweater, ironing her clothes, cooking, or even fixing her shoe, he was willing to do those things for her because it made her happy. Therefore, Bryan was also contributing to his own happiness because when she was happy, she would also do the things that make him happy. When you stroke your man's ego and let him be your Superman, he'll do the same thing for you even if he doesn't realize it!

✓ **FLIRT WITH YOUR MAN**

Many women complain that when they are out with their man, other women flirt with him. One way of avoiding this is to flirt with him yourself. If you are the one doing the flirting, then maybe he won't notice when another woman attempts to flirt with him.

Wink at him, compliment him, hold his hand, and be affectionate. If you don't, there will be plenty of others who might!

✓ Be Into What He's Into

A great bedroom relationship is a wonderful thing, but sooner or later, you have to step out into the world. Develop some interest in music or sports so that you can have something else to talk about outside of the bedroom. In order for him to stay interested, you've got to have something in common.

✓ Most Men are Asset Men

Men are more attracted to someone who they perceive as an asset, not a liability. If you want to be thought of this way, you must have *some* financial independence. A good man will not expect you to take care of him, but he will find it attractive if you are capable of being financially secure.

✓ Be Strong and Independent — Not Clingy and Dependent

While it's okay to be interested in the same things as your man, be sure you also have your own interests and hobbies. It is important to have a life of your own other than the one you share with him. Don't lose yourself in order to be with a man.

For six months, Jackie, a twenty-five-year-old loan officer from Atlanta, had been dating Greg, a hip-hop artist. Jackie was beginning to feel that Greg no longer showed her the attention he used to. She heard rumors that he had been seen around town at different events with other women. He broke dates and sometimes stood her up when they had made plans. Jackie knew in her heart that she needed to end the relationship, but she enjoyed the perks of being connected with such a well-known man. Just the association with his name allowed her to go to the finest restaurants and clubs, and she was considered VIP because she was his girl. She knew that if she left Greg, she would lose her status. During their relationship Jackie structured her life to fit his; she took on his identity, and she felt that if she were no longer with him, she wouldn't be able to go back to her own identity because she couldn't even remember who she was before she met Greg.

When you remain true to yourself and continue to be you, a man will have to love and accept you for who you are, not who he wants you to be.

✓ BE SEXUALLY OPEN AND CELEBRATE YOUR SEXUALITY

Ladies, whether you want to hear it or not, one of the greatest sexual acts for a man is oral sex. If you are good at performing this act, you won't have to worry about anything. I have yet to hear any man say he doesn't like the feel of his woman's mouth on his manhood, even if she is not all that good at it, which men define only as a lack of enthusiasm. In a sexual relationship, enthusiasm alone can turn a lackluster experience into a mind-blowing experience, but there is an art to being good at orally satisfying a man. However, if you don't enjoy it, you'd better believe your man will know. So, in order to keep a sexually fulfilled man, don't just *act* like you enjoy it, but *learn* to enjoy it. Turning a man on orally is a powerful feeling. You are in total control. Ask your man to share with you what he wants and what feels good to him. Every man is different, and what feels good to one may not be as enjoyable to another. Men are much less complicated than women and can be pleased quite easily once you know what they want.

The most important thing that will almost always guarantee you getting a husband is to not just make your man feel like *the* man, but allow him to actually *be* the man. We are living in a day and time where women can do most anything a man can do. We pay our own bills, we work full-time jobs, take care of our homes and our children, many of us earn higher salaries than the man in our life, however, women must comprehend that for men, the greatest feeling in the world is to be recognized and appreciated for who they are: MEN. You have to know what *he* wants, and sometimes in order to achieve the results *you* want, you have to make him feel as if it was his idea.

Calling it Quits
(When Mr. Right is 'so' wrong)

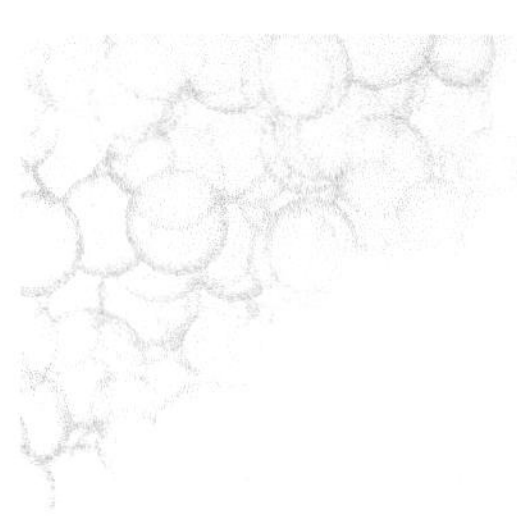

adies, there are some men out there who just won't commit. In many cases, it's not because he is afraid of commitment, but he might not want to commit to you. If you have been in a long-term relationship (longer than a year) and your man is not showing any signs of making his way to the altar, and if you have followed all the rules outlined in the previous chapter and you haven't achieved results, you have to know when to walk away. It is up to a woman to draw the line when she sees that the relationship is not progressively moving forward. A man can and will continue to string you along *if* you allow it!

If a man sees that he can continue to have sex with you without a commitment, you better believe he will continue to do so. Even today, men are not in the habit of buying the cow when they can get the milk for free. Men ask themselves, *"Why should I bother marrying her if we're already living together and acting married?"* Most men will be more than happy to take all the benefits without the expensive ring and those pesky little vows.

Women know when they are stuck in a stagnant relationship, yet most feel powerless to take action to rectify the situation. Women often say, "I know he's not good for me, but how do I move on?" It is never easy to end a relationship, whether you have been in it for six months or sixty years. However, you must recognize that the relationship is truly over before you can move on and start healing.

There are a number of reasons why women stay in dead-end relationships, and one of those reasons is great sex. The other is lack of self-confidence or low self-esteem, but first, let's talk about sex.

It is a common misconception that women do not like sex. In fact, women quickly become addicted to great sex. Women know that sometimes it can be difficult to find exceptional mind-blowing sex, so when we find that man who has the ability to provide us with one Earth-shattering orgasm after another; we will cling to him as if our very existence depends on him. It doesn't matter that the rest of the relationship is not working. It doesn't matter that you are giving up too much of yourself, your time, your money — whatever your situation may be. But it does matter, ladies! You MUST learn to let go of unhealthy, toxic relationships. When you realize you are stuck in a dead-end relationship that is not progressively moving forward, you must let it go.

Sometimes, it is not so much the man we are unwilling to let go of. Rather, it is our fixation on his penis. That's right, ladies. We can and often are addicted to his penis. Sex *is* an addiction for some people — maybe not for everyone, but just like gambling, drugs, alcohol, and cigarettes, sex can be addictive. Unlike some addictions, like cigarettes and alcohol, for instance, you can't slowly wean yourself off sex. It's either all or nothing. You will never be able to get out of bed with a man that you love and have absolutely the best sex with and say, "That was amazing, but I'm so over you now." So, in order to separate yourself from a good penis, you must quit cold turkey, with no contact whatsoever, no visits, no texts, no emails, and no phone calls. You have to get rid of everything that reminds you of him, erase all those old messages you saved on your answering machine, and pack up all the pictures and other personal items he's left behind.

You have to find something that symbolizes the end for you. Maybe you can have a burial ceremony for all the mementoes, pictures, and keepsakes that remind you of him and your relationship. If it helps you to heal, do it. One of my girlfriends has taken to tossing her memories of her ex's in the ocean. She says that once it's done, she feels free. I, on the other hand, finalize my relationships by tossing my ex's toothbrush in the trash. It is the last step after everything has been boxed up or thrown away. Once that toothbrush hits the trash, I know it is really over and there is no going back. It symbolizes our relationship: in the trash.

Just as it is easy to backslide when seeking treatment for drug and alcohol abuse, it is also easy to backslide when trying to get over a good penis, so you need a buddy support system. After a breakup, it is common to have moments of weakness when we start second-guessing ourselves, wondering if we made the right decision. When we reminisce about the happier times in our relationship, we begin to itch and ache to pick up the phone just to hear his voice. Don't do it! It will only end up a booty call, and afterwards, you will find yourself in an even bigger mess because now he knows your weakness is in his pants. This is why it is important to have a buddy support system. Your buddy will always remind you of the reason you broke up in the first place.

Also, while trying to separate yourself from a good penis, you may experience what I call Penis Withdrawal Symptoms (PWS). You may feel a quiver of lust or the proverbial butterflies in the pit of your stomach when thoughts of him cross your mind or maybe when you see something that reminds you of him like his favorite cologne, television program, or maybe the restaurant where you've celebrated special occasions. These symptoms are temporary and will eventually go away. In order to minimize these symptoms, it is important to keep busy. Keeping busy is one of the best remedies known for getting over a man and a bad case of PWS. Get involved in activities that keep your mind occupied. Take up a new hobby.

One of those new hobbies might be to start dating again. There is truth in the saying that the best way to get over one man is to get with another. Although it is important to give yourself time to heal before getting involved in a serious relationship, there is nothing wrong with harmless casual dating, so go out and have some fun. When your man sees that you have moved on, he may try any and everything to get you back. A man who is really into you will not be able to tolerate the thought of you being with someone else, but don't let this sudden renewed interest in you take you off course. He is probably only interested because he knows another is moving in on what he considers to be his territory, and his ego is bruised.

Ladies, we must stop making it so easy for men to use us. When you meet a man, don't immediately jump between the sheets with him. Give yourself time to see if you still want him after the alcohol wears off. Some women have a problem recognizing the difference between a real relationship and a fling. Oftentimes, women have sex with a man first and then question if she is in a relationship. Establish parameters before you give up the goods! Take time to allow a man to get into your head and your heart before you allow him into your body. Take some time and listen closely to the things he is telling you. The more you listen, the more you learn what type of man he really is. Learning the truth about a man can help you stop being hurt by someone who couldn't possibly love you. If a man is not interested in having a relationship, his actions will usually tell you within the first few dates, even if he doesn't say it aloud. A lot of times, we already know the answer, but we are not willing to see and accept it.

Recognize the warning signs that the relationship is not going to become what you want it to become. Warning signs are *always* there. Most of the time, we either choose to ignore them or make excuses for them, but if you carefully evaluate the situation, it should be easy to recognize the obvious.

The other reason women may hesitate to end a dead-end relationship is lack of self-confidence or low self-esteem. Every woman suffers from low self-esteem at some point in her life, and some men enjoy using a woman's negative self-image to their advantage. Your man may try to convince you that you are not good enough to find someone who will treat you better. He may also tell you he is the best thing that ever happened to you, and if your self-esteem is low, you just might believe him (though if he's the kind of man who would tell you that, you most definitely CAN find someone better than him).

I once dated a man who was way too critical of me. Whenever we were together, I would catch him studying me — not looking at me appreciatively, but critically. If he saw even one strand of gray hair, he would say, "It's time for some Clairol."

To begin with, I was always nervous around this man. I couldn't relax and enjoy myself because I was constantly checking my appearance. Eventually, I began to ignore him when I saw him studying me. I knew I looked good, and all he ever did was criticize. No matter how attractive I looked, he would always find something negative to say. I began to realize he was happiest when he could make me feel down about myself.

After about six weeks of this treatment, I'd had enough and ended the relationship. It is not love when someone tries to pick your self-esteem apart. If your man enjoys treating you this way, it is not because there is something wrong with you — there is something wrong with *him*. If you are with someone who is overly critical and never has anything good to say to you or about you, it may be time to re-evaluate your relationship.

Another reason some women may hesitate to end a dead-end relationship is fear of being labeled a failure. After you have bragged to your friends and family about how wonderful your man is, it can be difficult to suddenly say, "Oops, I made a mistake! Mr. Wonderful isn't so wonderful anymore." So in some cases rather than look like a failure some women would rather endure an unhealthy relationship even though her needs are not being met.

Do not at any time think you can change a man. Karol, a thirty-eight-year-old attorney, said her man of four years refuses to talk about taking their relationship to the next level. When it comes to discussing marriage, he says he is not ready for that type of commitment yet. "But I'm hoping I can change his mind," Karol says.

What this man is really saying to Karol is, "I'm not ready to commit to YOU!" Ladies, it doesn't take years for a man to know if he wants you as his wife, so don't allow him to keep you hanging on for an indefinite amount of time while he waits to see if someone better is going to come along. If he tells you he's not ready, accept him at his word and remove yourself from the relationship. Don't hang in there thinking you will eventually wear him down and convince him to change his mind.

Ladies, the only change you have control over are the ones you make in yourselves. You can change your behavior and your way of thinking. Set boundaries so you know what you can and cannot tolerate, and don't let the men in your life cross those boundaries, period.

For example, if a man asks me out and we agree that he will pick me up at seven p.m., I allow him a twenty-minute grace period. If I don't see or hear from him within this twenty minutes, I forget the date and go about my business. If he arrives after this twenty-minute period, I have no problem telling him the date is off and I am no longer available. If you don't want to be there if and when he arrives, leave. Most men feel dejected when they finally show up at seven thirty expecting you to be ready and waiting and you're not at home. He will most likely call your cellular phone to find out where you are. I respond as sweetly as possible, "I'm sorry. When you didn't call or show by seven twenty, I assumed you changed your mind and made other plans, so I did too. Maybe we can get together some other time."

This is not a game. However, it is one way that men will realize that you must be taken seriously. You better believe that in the future, if he is running late, he will pick up the phone and call. Why? Because he knows if he doesn't you won't be there.

If there is something you need and want out of a relationship that you're not getting, don't settle! My girlfriend Kristin has been involved with her man for seven years. They have one child together. Kristin constantly complains that she hasn't been satisfied with her relationship for a long time. She loves her man and wants to be his wife. She has no desire to be with anyone else, but she is unhappy in her current situation. After seven years, there is still no sign of improvement in the relationship. She says her man neglects her and is insensitive to her feelings. "We never spend any time together other than when he comes over to have sex, but he always manages to spend time engaged in other social activities with his buddies. He is always jumping on a plane and taking a trip somewhere, yet he never includes me. I just want some quality time! I would love for us to take the kids to Disney World, but he feels I should just be happy that he is financially taking care of us," she said.

You may think that if you are good enough to a man, he will change, but we have to face the facts. As we've already learned, you cannot change a man. It is better to accept the fact that you may have to just move on so that you can be available when you do meet that potential Mr. Right who is ready to commit. Learn to love yourself and realize that failed relationships provide us with an opportunity to learn and grow so that we are able to look forward and be open to accept love.

Learn to Love the Body You're In

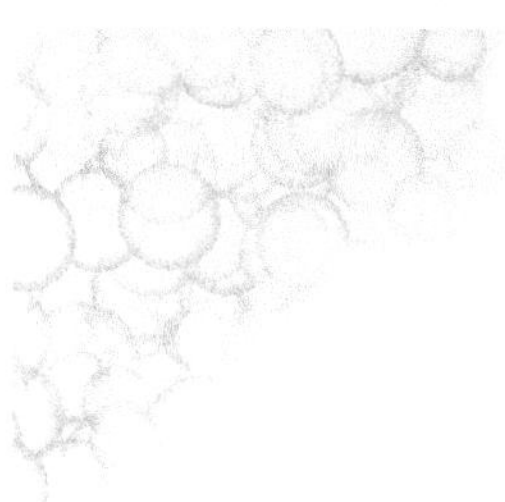

The older I get, the wiser I get. I consider myself absolutely fabulous at 44. I am more confident and secure about my body now than when I was in my twenties. When I weighed 125 pounds, I was very insecure and self-conscious about my body. I wasn't happy with my appearance. My butt wasn't big enough, and my boobs were too small. Now, a couple decades later, my body has definitely gone through some drastic changes due to surgical scars and weight gain.

It is easy to allow insecurities to prevent you from enjoying a fulfilling sex life. Men are not as conscious about the physical aspects of the body as we think. As I stated earlier, men do love nice bodies and pretty faces, but they define 'pretty' as sexy. Think about it... how many times have you seen the other woman and wondered, *what is he doing with her when his wife is so much prettier?* Men love desirable women, and these women appeal to his sexual side. I listen to many women complain that they hate to undress in front of their man because of a little extra weight, stretch marks, and saggy breasts. Most men really don't care about those trivial details. As I said before, men are looking for fantasy and how you view yourself can make a huge difference in how he perceives you. If you carry yourself with confidence and exhibit your sensuality he will find you absolutely irresistible.

Several years ago at the age of thirty-six, I was diagnosed with breast cancer. I had just divorced my third husband five months prior to being diagnosed. I had a mastectomy of my right breast, and went through six months of chemotherapy (which made my hair fall completely out) followed by six weeks of radiation. Believe me when I say my body was not at its best, but during this time, I married for the fourth time. The man I married didn't care about the way my body looked. He saw past the scars and the bald head. No matter what my outward appearance, he still visualized me as a sexy, desirable woman. The image of the woman I was before my illness was etched into his brain, and I continued to reinforce that image by maintaining my sensuality.

Years ago, I worked as a weight loss counselor in a nationally known weight loss center. On a daily basis, I came in contact with many women who were dealing with self-esteem issues. One of my most memorable clients was Cindy, who weighed in at 321 pounds. Cindy also suffered from depression and other health problems such as high blood pressure and high cholesterol due to her weight. During our sessions, Cindy would often cry when she talked about how her family treated her because of her weight. Her children, a fifteen-year-old son and a twelve-year-old daughter were blatantly and publicly ashamed of her, so much so that they never wanted her to attend any of their school functions. Her daughter was a gymnast and was totally obsessed with sports. Cindy had overheard her daughter saying to her grandmother that she needed to stay active because she didn't want to end up looking like her mother.

Cindy's husband was extremely verbally abusive. He had several choice names for her, but his favorite was 'fat ugly slob', which he used quite frequently. He even refused to sleep in the same bed with her. Cindy knew her husband was cheating; he would often take other women's phone numbers while she was present. He also made fun of her in public, around friends and family members and even around her children. Cindy desired to lose the weight, but it seemed impossible, especially with no support from her family. She prepared healthy meals for her family, which she ate in moderate portions, but her husband would order pizza for him and the kids and then eat it right in front of her.

Cindy had even considered suicide but never followed through for fear of leaving her children without a mother. When Cindy came in to the center for her sessions, sometimes we would cry together. I could identify with a lot of what she was going through in dealing with her weight problems. Cancer treatments caused me to go from a normal weight of 145 pounds to 185 pounds, which was the biggest I had ever been in my life. Although I lost my extra unwanted pounds in a matter of sixteen weeks, Cindy had been living with her weight for years. I knew the pressure of wanting to see immediate results; I also understood the disappointment when it didn't happen. Anyone who has ever tried to lose weight can identify with the struggle. Cindy was also an emotional eater, so anytime she was going through any emotion (anger, sadness, boredom), she would eat. It was a habit she had been living with for years.

The first thing Cindy realized she had to do was separate herself from any negative energy in her life, her husband in particular. She developed new eating habits and started filling her days with new activities. Instead of eating, she went for long walks on the beach, which gave her time to reflect on the positive things in her life. It was a long, hard journey, but like anything else, when you invest time and energy into personal goals that you have set, it becomes a habit.

Eighteen months later, Cindy weighed 215 pounds. She is healthier and happier … and that pizza-eating, criticizing ex of hers wants to be part of the family again.

Your Health is Your Responsibility

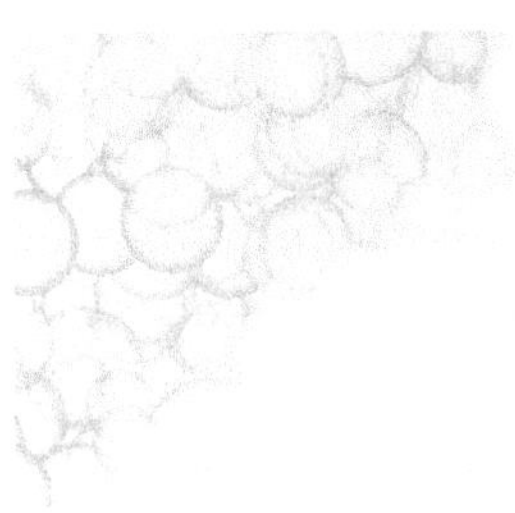

Nothing upsets me more than when I hear women complaining about health issues but refusing to go and get proper medical treatment. In spite of medical advancements, major health problems such as heart disease, cancer, and diabetes are occurring more frequently in the younger generation of women.

In the course of writing this book, I wanted to know how women, in general, feel about their health. So, one of the questions I asked women was "When was your last physical examination?"

Most women could not remember, and the ones who could only went for an exam when they were having a specific problem. You should have an annual physical examination at least once a year. If you notice any unusual changes in your body, go see your health care provider immediately. Don't wait, and do not try to diagnose and treat yourself. Sometimes early detection and treatment can save your life.

In September 2001, one week after my thirty-sixth birthday, I was getting out of the shower and going through my daily ritual of moisturizing my body with body oil. I was looking at my reflection in the mirror, and I could see where the impressions of my bra straps were starting to cut into my skin. My first thought was that I needed to apply cocoa butter to this area in order to fade these markings. While massaging the coco butter into my skin, as I reached my right underarm area, I felt a hard, solid lump, about the size of a small robin egg. In order to feel this lump, my arm had to be extended backward, as if I were trying to reach behind me. In any other position, I couldn't feel it. All my life from a very early age, I have been doing breast self-exams, and I had never previously detected anything abnormal with my breast. As I was saying, in order to feel this hard, solid mass, my arm had to be in an unusual position. Immediately, I became alarmed. It was after five o' clock in the evening, and the medical centers were already closed for the day. The first thing the following morning, I went to see my family physician. After he examined me, he sent me to a surgeon at one of the local hospitals.

With the location of this mass, it was extremely hard to detect, so the surgeon sent me for an ultrasound. At the completion of my examination, my surgeon advised me that whatever it was, it needed to be removed. My biopsy was scheduled for the following week.

In the days prior to my surgery I talked to many people. I spoke to many women who reassured me that it was probably nothing. Some had also had minor surgeries for cysts of the breast, so by the time my surgery date arrived, I was feeling quite confident that it was nothing — that they would remove the lump, and everything was going to be alright. When I checked into the hospital, my family was with me. I remember laughing with them about how hungry I was because I couldn't eat anything after midnight the night prior, and it was already after twelve thirty p.m. the next day.

My surgeon, Dr. Matthews, was the absolute best. I felt so relaxed and comfortable in his care. After I was given my 'happy medicine', the last thing I remember was him taking my hand and saying a prayer. When I came to, I was back in my private room, surrounded by my family. I was starving to death and ready to be discharged. I was mid-conversation with my mother when the doctor walked in. There was a look on his face, and I just knew. "Cancer," he said. "A very aggressive strain of invasive cancer. The lump we removed was about four inches in diameter." They also removed thirty-nine lymph nodes, nine of which tested positive for cancer.

Learning I had cancer was the most terrifying moment in my life. My whole world crumbled in a matter of seconds. I was in shock. I was lying on the hospital bed, but I remember looking behind me to see who the doctor was talking to because he couldn't possibly be talking to me. I had never been sick a day in my life, so how could I have cancer? I was crying so hard, and so was my family. I was angry and hurt. I had always tried to live right and treat people right, so I didn't understand why this was happening to me. I kept asking over and over, "Lord, why me? What did I do to deserve this?" I knew I could possibly die from this disease, but if I didn't die from the cancer, how was I ever going to survive the treatments?

As if through a fog, I could hear my surgeon talking about treatments; a mastectomy of my right breast, then chemotherapy, the strongest available based on the aggressiveness of my cancer. This would be followed by a solid six weeks of radiation, and because of my advanced stage, we needed to move fast. As I was being wheeled out of the hospital to my mother's vehicle, I was still in tears. Strangers passing in the halls stopped and gave me hugs without knowing my situation, but they saw the anguish and fear on my face.

My mother took me home with her and helped me to bed, where I cried myself to sleep. In my sleep, the Lord visited me. His presence was with me. Over and over again, I questioned Him. "Lord, why me?"

After some time, His reply was, "Why *not* you? You are the strength in this family. Your sister or your mother would not be able to go through this with your strength. You, my child, will be okay, and I will never leave your side."

Those were the last tears I ever cried for my illness. When I woke up, I was smiling, I was comforted, and I was happy. My mother thought I had lost my mind because the change was so instantaneous. I was happy because it was true: I knew I could never watch my mother or my sister go through this because it would hurt too much, so I was glad it was me. From that point on, whenever I thought about my disease, I actually thanked God. I thanked Him for being my strength, for I knew He would never leave me as I went through my journey with breast cancer.

A few weeks later, I had a mastectomy. Four weeks after that, I began chemotherapy. I married my fourth husband three days prior to starting chemotherapy. Three weeks after my first treatment, my hair started falling out in bunches. Although the doctors and nurses had informed me of what to expect, to watch it happen was still shocking. My husband shaved my head and then shaved his own. Fortunately, I continued to be blessed during my treatments. I never had any side effects from my chemotherapy treatment; I never got sick, and true to His word, I made it!

What Every Man Should Know About Women

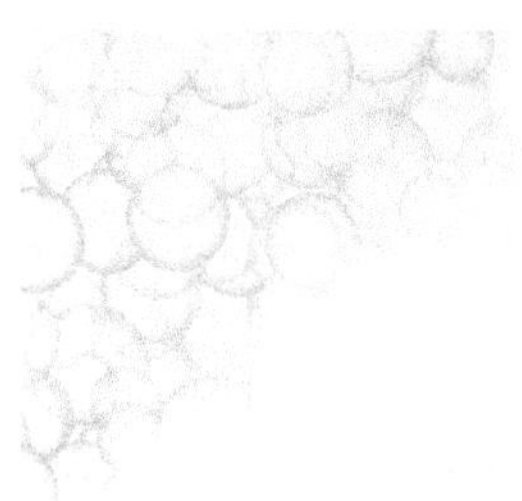

elationships begin to fail when there is a breakdown of intimacy within the relationship.

Therefore, in order to be successful, relationships need nurturing on an everyday basis. The diction-
ary defines *nurture* as: '*to care for, feed, nourish*'. This is
exactly what it takes to build successful, healthy relationships. You must invest time and effort into keeping
the passion and excitement alive in your relationship.

Men, it's time we talk to you. It is time to put the
same energy and effort into maintaining your relationship that you did when you were trying to win
your woman's affection. You should take an active
role in keeping your relationship exciting. Put yourself back into the relationship because many of you
have disconnected.

✓ PAY ATTENTION, MISTER!

Ladies, know that men are conquerors. The challenge
for a man is in winning you. In order to achieve his
mission, he will wine you, dine you, and woo you
with sweet words of love. He will promise to cherish
you, but as soon as he realizes you are his — heart,
soul, and body — he knows he can relax. After all,

his work is done, right? Wrong! Men, women love attention as much as you, and if you want a happy, fulfilled, satisfied woman, you need to step up *your* game. Women love thoughtful, considerate, loving men, and that is something every man has the potential to be. If you want your lady to go all out and give you the love and attention that you want, consider her feelings as well.

✓ Don't Just Wham Bam Your Ma'am!

Be sexually giving with your woman. I am here to set the record straight. It is time to start listening to what pleases your woman in bed. Men say we don't tell them about our sexual needs and wants, but that is not always true. I speak from experience when I say that in my lifetime, I have done more than my share of faking an orgasm. Why do women fake it? The reason is quite common, and it's simple: Most of the time, faking it is easier than dealing with a man's bruised ego when he thinks we are just trying to find one more thing to complain about.

It took time and a special breed of man to make me realize that I deserve to be sexually satisfied. We women give our bodies with our hearts, and we deserve to get what we give and no less. It is not just a physical connection for us. We require more! In the course of writing this book, I have talked to many women about the lack of intimacy within their relationships. Recently, at a book event, a woman asked me "How important is sex in a relationship?"

I replied, "It depends on who you ask." Men place more importance on sex because it is one of his basic needs. Although sex is not a primary importance for women, most will agree that intimacy with their partner plays an important role in how they relate to their partner.

Many women complain that there is a lack of emotional stimulation during sexual intercourse. "He gets up there, does his thing, and a few minutes later, he is done," says one woman. Some said having sex with their partner was equivalent to going to the gym. One woman even said, "I have never been in so many positions in so few minutes. Sometimes, I feel like I'm taking part in a workout routine."

Most men are surprised to learn that many women have never had an orgasm during the actual act of intercourse. Some men don't know how to stimulate their woman or how they want to be touched. Men respond to this by saying, "Sometimes it takes women too long to reach an orgasm." I agree, because if you don't know what a woman wants, you're not going to know what it takes to bring her to an orgasm. It is just as much your responsibility to talk to your woman, watch her response to what you are doing, and ask what her needs are. Just because she is moaning doesn't mean she is enjoying it; she could be in pain.

Most men seem to think they are great in bed. This is what I call an over-inflated ego. The really strange thing about sex is that you assume your partner knows what you want. Ladies, you have to find a way to express your needs to your partner without damaging his self-esteem. You also have to discover how to have an orgasm while making love. If there is something you need that you're not getting, speak up! Any discussions about problems dealing with sexual issues should be addressed outside the bedroom, in a manner that will not further damage his or your self-esteem.

The primary complaint that I frequently hear from women is that men don't spend enough time with foreplay. Foreplay, gentlemen, is an ongoing experience. Foreplay begins between a woman's ears, not between her legs. Foreplay starts when the day begins, and it doesn't just have to take place in the bedroom before the actual act. Foreplay consists of a variety of things. If your lady is in the kitchen cooking dinner for the family and you walk up, embrace her from behind, and kiss her on the cheek; that is foreplay. Giving her a call during your workday just to tell her that you're thinking of her and can't wait to get home is foreplay. Any gesture that shows sensitivity, love, caring, genuine interest, and affection is foreplay — a prelude to what is to come.

✓ Tell Her Everything's Gonna Be Alright

If you know your lady is stressed, the best thing you can do is show her that you understand. Be considerate and do something special to show her you are there for her and that you are willing to be her strength when she needs you. Alleviate some of the stress from her life. If it means taking the kids so she can have some alone time, do it, and allow her that time. This will show her that you care about her well-being, and it will be worth it to you in the long run. Remember, when she's happy, you will be happy. Give her a spa day, pamper her, and make her feel like the queen that she is. Do something out of the ordinary. Take her on a romantic picnic in the park or at the beach. When I'm having a bad day, the thing that endears me to my man is that he listens. He doesn't try to minimize my problems, and he doesn't try to offer solutions to solve my problem. He simply listens and encourages me, and then he may do something silly such as sing his own rendition of Bob Marley's "Don't Worry." The point is, he makes me smile. No matter how big the problem is, my man makes me feel like everything *is* going to be alright.

✓ WE'RE NOT ALL MATERIAL GIRLS

Guys, most women are really not as materialistic as you may think. A lot can be said by just being yourself when you meet a lady that you may be interested in. We don't want you to impress us with your success, what type of car you drive, what you do for a living, or how much money you make. Yes, we do need to know that you are able to be a provider and that you are marriage material, but the same is true for you. When you select a woman, it is always best to look deeper than what is on the surface. If you are looking for a trophy woman — just a big ol' chunk of eye candy to show off to your buds — that is exactly the kind of woman you're going to attract. But remember … trophies come at a price.

Romantic Things Women Love

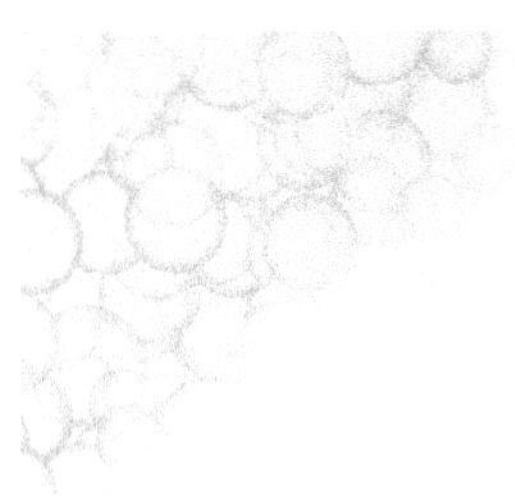

have included this chapter because I feel it's important to let men know what women consider romance. I can't begin to tell you the number of times men have confessed to not knowing what to do for their woman, so here are some suggestions for you fellas:

✓ Picnic It

Take your lady on a picnic in the park or at the beach. Depending on where you live, you can even create the same romantic effect in your own backyard. All you need is a blanket, a few sandwiches, maybe some fruit (chocolate-dipped strawberries are great), and a bottle of champagne, and you're set! Quality quiet time together is important, so even if it's not your thing, act like you're enjoying your-self … because your lady will be enjoying you.

✓ Sunup and Sundown

Take your woman to a beach or a natural spot with a great view of the sunset or sunrise. Take along a bottle of her favorite champagne or wine, and bask in the awe of nature and of time together.

Be Sweet to Her Feet. It is so erotic for many women to watch a man handle her feet. Give your lady a manicure or pedicure, or if you don't feel talented enough for this sort of thing, massage her feet and paint her toenails for her.

✓ GET TOUCHY-FEELY

Touching, touching, and more touching, please! Physical contact such as hugging, and holding hands is extremely important to your woman. Touching is sensual … and it is essential.

✓ SHOW A LITTLE PDA

Not only do we women enjoy knowing that we are loved and cherished, but we want others to know it as well. Many years ago, I had just started dating a new man. One day, while I was on the job, he sent me a different flower arrangement every hour on the hour, for my full nine-hour shift. It was the talk of my building, and it made me the envy of every woman there. At the end of the day, he showed up like my knight in shining armor to help me get my beautiful garden of florals home. So go ahead and send those flowers to her at work! Your lady will love you for it … and she'll be flattered by the jealous looks she'll get.

✓ GET A LITTLE CLICHÉ

It might sound old-hat or cliché, but there is a reason candlelight dinners are so popular. Prepare a nice candle-light dinner for your lady, complete with wine, flowers, and soothing, sensual music. If you can't cook, hire someone to do it for you, or pick up some take-out from her favorite restaurant and put it on some beautiful china to serve to her.

✓ MAKE THE THOUGHT WORTH COUNTING

On special occasions such as her birthday, your milestone anniversaries, or Valentine's Day, give her personal gifts of love — and skip the practical stuff. I will never forget when a man I dated years ago gave me a vacuum cleaner for Valentine's Day! It was a very expensive model, but as far as gifts go … well, it sucked! And I even had hardwood floors!

When it comes to gift giving, sometimes it means more when you do something out of the ordinary. Everyone sends candy, flowers, and balloons. These are traditional gifts, and during certain occasions, your woman may already suspect what you are going to give, so do something to give these gifts your own special touch. For example, in a previous relationship, the man I was dating wasn't big on gift giving. So, on every special occasion, I knew what he was giving me was green and one-size-fits-all: money, often between $1,000 and $1,500! He was very consistent. Now, don't get me wrong, money is good, but I sat down and expressed that it would make me happy if he put just a little bit more thought into his gifts. The following Valentine's Day, I arrived home to find a beautiful stuffed bear on the bar. Attached to the bear were ten balloons in pink, white, and red, and inside each balloon was a one-hundred-dollar bill. I was impressed not so much because of the money, but because he found a way to make it extra special.

✓ A Good Thing Never Really Dies

Always be a gentleman and chivalrous. Contrary to popular belief, chivalry is not dead! So, open those doors, pull out her chair, and hold her hand. Help her into and out of a vehicle. This behavior displays that she is special, and it sends the message that you are proud she's with you.

✓ Wash, Rinse, Repeat

One thing you might not think of is washing your woman's hair. This is a very sensuous experience for a woman, but keep in mind that it might not be the perfect scenario if your woman wears hairpieces, wigs, or extensions. Most African-American women would rather you keep your hands out of her hair, so as an alternative, you can give body massages and a good hand massage.

✓ THE LANGUAGE OF LOVE

Remember when you were in high school, and you made fun of that guy who sat around writing poetry? Well, that guy might be your hero when it comes to impressing your lady. Read stories or poems of love in bed. Better yet, read to her from the best love letter ever written — the Bible.

✓ SPLISH SPLASH

As nice as it is to draw a warm bath for your lady after she's had a long, hard day, you can one-up that deal by actually *giving* her a bath and joining her in one, washing every inch of her body. Create a special, private oasis just for her. Run a bath surrounded with her favorite scented candles. Add her favorite bath salts or bubble bath, complete with a glass of wine. Allow her to relax and unwind, uninterrupted, and then finish it off with a sensual body massage. Nothing turns me on more than when I am in the tub and my man comes in with candles, slowly undresses, and gets in the bath with me. Need I say more?

✓ KEEP YOUR DISTANCE

Like you, sometimes your woman will get moody for seemingly no apparent reason. During these times, don't press her for information or make matters worse by hovering or demanding explanations or fussing over her too much. Allow your woman her space and give her some time, and eventually, things will return to normal.

✓ Something's Gotta Give

Every relationship requires give and take. You won't always want to let your woman have her way, but you can't always have yours either. You have to be willing to find a happy medium, pick your battles, and compromise a little. Tiny sacrifices make a big impression that she'll remember.

✓ Saying "I'm Sorry"

Don't be afraid or too stubborn to apologize. There is no weakness in being wrong, but you gain so much respect for being man enough to admit when you are. I know firsthand that sometimes it helps to apologize even when you know you didn't do anything wrong, just to get back to normal.

✓ No Night Fights

It has been said many times that a couple should never go to bed mad, and this is a true sentiment. When you go to bed angry, holding negative feelings inside, not only does it prevent you from getting a restful night's sleep, but it also allows you to subconsciously hold on to the anger. You will probably stay on your side of the bed, curled in a fetal position, making it clear that you don't want to be touched. If you make this behavior a habit, subconsciously your brain begins to tell you that you really don't want to be touched, so it's best to resolve any issues before going to sleep.

✓ You Can Never Say It Enough

Always — and I mean ALWAYS — say "Thank you," and this works both ways. It may sound silly, but it really works. I don't care if my man does something as trivial as taking out the trash, washing my car, or paying bills; even if it's his responsibility, I always thank him. I say it so often I sometimes find my man looking for something else to do, and he doesn't even realize it. Chances are, your lady does a lot for you because she wants to and feels responsible to, but be sure you thank her for it anyway.

✓ Don't Take Her For Granted

Be attentive to your partner. The quickest way to drive your woman into the arms (and bed) of another man or that standby of hers is to neglect her. When one man stops paying attention, another man is always willing to give that attention. If your woman changes her hair, you should notice that. If she loses weight, tell her she looks good — heck, tell her that even if she gains a little. Let her know that you appreciate all the hard work she is doing to look good for you. This will encourage her to take better care of herself. Other ways to remember her are to call her from work and ask how her day is going or tell her you love her, or you can even turn off the television when she talks (and yes, EVEN during a playoff game if that's what your relationship needs). Make a point of cuddling or being affectionate without being sexual. Treat her with the same attention you did in the beginning of your relationship, and she will never feel neglected enough to run to another man.

✓ **Don't Be a Dirty Boy**

Always wash before having sex. While many men complain about things their women will not do in bed, what they do not realize is that some of her hesitation might be eliminated if you practice better personal hygiene. So guys, keep it together and make good personal hygiene a priority. Surely, you want your woman clean and fresh, so keep in mind that she needs and deserves the same from you. No lady wants motor oil all over the silky nightie she's wearing for you or to be fondled with grubby hands!

✓ **Just the Two of Us**

If you truly want to show your lady how special she is, create special times to be alone together. Take her on a short romantic getaway or weekend trip, and don't forget to make all the arrangements for the babysitter as well.

✓ **Just Do It**

Do necessary chores around the house without being asked. Guys, we are not your mamas! We should NOT have to tell you to do what you already know has to be done, and having to ask puts us in the awkward position of having to feel like a nag or admitting we need help. If you drive up in the driveway and see that the grass is high, we shouldn't have to break down three weeks later and ask you to handle that. You know what your responsibilities are and what you're supposed to do as a MAN, so just do it!

✓ Be Fine

It is just as important for you to look good for your woman as it is for her to look good for you. When dressing for a night out, take extra pains with your appearance. Make her proud to show you off. And while you're at it, don't forget to smell sexy! Nothing turns me on like the masculine scent of cologne. Scents delight our sensual side, and any woman will love it when her man smells yummy!

✓ Only Have Eyes for Her

When you are out together — or even if you're sitting in your living room watching a television show saturated with bikini-clad dancers or volleyball players — treat your woman like she is the only woman in the room. Women are instinctively self-critical, and she doesn't need you making her feel less attractive than anyone. This type of affection will help you retain a healthy emotional connection with your lady.

Ladies, remember that these guidelines are for healthy relationships, and all the things I suggested for the men apply in reverse as well. Sometimes we forget to show how much we love and appreciate our men — with the exception of painting his nails, perhaps!

The Hands-Off Rule

Frankly, as women, we need to adopt a 'Hands-Off Rule'. This simply means we need to keep our grubby little hands off of anyone else's man. It took a long time for me to learn a lesson about dating married men, having been involved with them on more than one occasion. The longest relationship lasted for a year. In my early twenties, after my first marriage ended, I was involved with a man named Justin. During this year, Justin continuously promised me he was leaving his wife … and naïve as I was, I believed him.

In the meantime, his wife knew about me, and we made each others' lives a living hell. Due to Justin's carelessness, his wife found my phone number. So, I got the normal hang-up calls as well as the late-night drives past my house, whenever she decided to check and see if he was there. At this point in our relationship, Justin no longer cared that his wife knew about his affair, so he told her about me, but he wouldn't end his relationship with me, and he wouldn't divorce her. During the times she was out of the country (which were frequent), it was common for me to stay with Justin at their home. When she called, I answered the phone and was more than happy to let her know I was in her home before I passed the phone to Justin. After the call, he always asked why I had to aggravate her. This insanity went on for a year.

Justin's next-door neighbors were three beautiful, blonde, blue-eyed young ladies. Whenever I was there, I noticed they were a little too familiar, too casual with *my* Justin. I have taught myself to always observe what is going on around me, and whenever I was at Justin's home, I noticed these three young ladies would smile, giggle, and flirt with him.

One day, I decided to ask Justin if anything sexual had ever taken place between him and his neighbors. After convincing him that I wouldn't be upset and I only wanted the truth, he reluctantly admitted that one of the women had once knocked on his door. When he answered the door, he saw that she was in her bathrobe, but it was common for them to sometimes stop by and ask to borrow items such as sugar, eggs, milk, or whatever, so he let her in. Inside, she opened her bathrobe to reveal a skimpy two-piece bikini and asked his opinion on how it looked. Justin admitted he was speechless. His neighbor took this as a sign of approval and unhooked her bikini top and let it fall to the floor. When he didn't respond, she slowly stepped out of the bikini bottoms. Justin got an erection. She noticed it, came toward him, unzipped his pants, dropped to her knees, and started to suck his dick.

I asked what he was doing while she was sucking his dick, and Justin said, "Nothing. I didn't even touch her. My hands were behind my back." Then he said, "I didn't touch her because I would never cheat on you."

I was so disgusted and angry, but it finally hit me, and I responded that he could never cheat on *me*; he was already cheating on his *wife*. I ended my relationship with Justin that day, and I never looked back.

Justin was enjoying having his cake and eating it, too, and I learned from that painful and embarrassing incident not to ever let a man devalue me for his own gain and sexual gratification.

I later met Eric, a forty-seven-year-old corporate executive from Atlanta. On our first date, Eric told me he was married, but his wife was terminally ill, and her doctors didn't expect her to live through the year. Needless to say, this was our first and last date. I don't know if what Eric told me about his wife's heart condition was true, but I do know that married is married. I made a conscious decision that I would not see, date, or sleep with someone else's man — that I would follow the Hands-Off Rule.

Do not allow yourself to be the other woman. It is my experience that either way you go when dealing with a married man, you lose. We sometimes justify our actions by thinking if we don't know the wife, that it is somehow okay, but it's not. Not only would you be hurting the wife and breaking up a family, but in the process, you'll also be hurting yourself. If the marriage was already over before you, he would already be divorced. Occasionally, a woman will convince a man to leave his wife, only to find out that when he does, he's really not what she wanted anyway. The challenge was in getting him to leave because, just like men, we often want what we can't have. Being with a married man is exciting and challenging until you actually have him. Then reality sets in, the challenge is gone, and you are left with a man that you know has a habit of cheating. The relationship begins to lose some of its luster, and the excitement starts to fade. Ladies, always remember that if a man is willing to leave his wife and family for you, he will leave you for someone else. When we learn to respect ourselves, men will give us the respect we deserve.

Protecting Our Children

learned about sex at a very early age, not from being physically sexually active, but by reading anything and everything pertaining to the subject. When I was eleven years old, I spent all of my meager allowance on *Cosmopolitan* magazines. In all the books and magazines, I kept reading about something called 'the Big O', and I wanted to know what it was. After much reading (and practice), I finally learned how to physically please myself at the age of thirteen. I think this was one of the things that kept me from actually experimenting with sexual intercourse with any of the fresh boys that I came into contact with in my neighborhood.

When I was fifteen, my stepfather often left pornographic videos and magazines lying around in the bathroom and on the kitchen table when no else was at home but me. I'm sure he knew I would look at them, but they were always moved by the time someone else showed up at home. He also had a habit of walking past my bedroom in the nude when no one else was at home but me. He would often say things like, "You sure are a sexy 'lil thing. One day, you're going to make some man a good woman."

I often wondered why he would have these conversations with me when no one else was around. I never said anything to my mother for fear that she would think I had said or done something to make him say these things to me. As a child, I also thought my imagination was making me think his actions were somewhat inappropriate. Years later, after I left home and joined the military, I had a conversation with my stepfather in which he stated he had always been attracted to me, even at an early age. He said that when I left home, there was no reason for him to continue to stay, so he left. I had always known there was no love between my mother and my stepfather. Actually, the only reason they married was so my mom could gain custody of my siblings and me after my mom and dad divorced.

I still have a lot of respect for my stepfather for taking on that responsibility, but my response to him was that I still continue to see him as a father figure, who was, at one point, closer to me than my biological father. Fortunately, my stepfather never crossed the line, and since he was a truck driver and spent a lot of time away from home, I compensated by staying away from him when he was home. I bring this up because a lot of teenage girls are not as fortunate as I was. It is your responsibility as a mother to protect your children, especially your daughters.

While in the Army I met Teresa, a forty-five-year-old divorcee and single mother. Teresa met and married for the second time when her daughter Mya was twelve years old. She married thirty-seven-year-old Troy. Teresa thought everything was great with her new family. Her daughter got along with her new stepfather seemingly well. They hung out together, they played, and they enjoyed being together as a family.

When Mya turned fourteen, her husband Troy suggested that maybe it was time to start thinking about getting Mya on some form of birth control. Teresa felt uneasy discussing this with Troy, but he convinced her that because Mya had taken an interest in some of the young boys she'd met at school and in the neighborhood it was the right thing to do. Teresa felt starting her daughter on birth control was condoning sexual activity, but after much consideration, she realized she would rather be safe than sorry. After many discussions with Mya and a trip to the clinic, Mya began taking birth control pills at age fourteen.

When Mya turned fifteen, Teresa claimed she got a funny feeling when she watched Mya with Troy. "I don't know what it was, but the body language wasn't quite right," she said. "Sometimes they would fall asleep on the sofa while watching television, Mya with her head on Troy's chest. Sometimes he was shirtless, and she would be in short shorts and a tight t-shirt. She seldom wore a bra, and her nipples were clearly visible. There were many times I would walk in on them laughing and whispering to each other. Once, I heard loud shrieks of laughter from the back yard. When I went out back to see what was going on, there she was on Troy's back. He was running around the yard giving her a piggyback ride. I yelled for him to put her down, and I could have sworn he had a hard-on. I wanted to believe I was imagining things, so I expressed my concerns to Troy. I told him that Mya was too old for him to be so playful with. Troy said I was overreacting and they were just having fun."

Teresa said she also had conversations with Mya. She let her know that she was growing up, her body was developing and it wasn't appropriate to dress or behave a certain way around any male, her stepfather included.

One night at about two a.m., while working the late shift, Teresa was bothered by something she couldn't explain, but she felt the need to go home early. When she arrived, she didn't pull into the garage as she normally did. Instead, she parked on the street. She entered the house through the back door, and all was quiet except for the sound of a television somewhere in the house. She continued down the hallway where she reached her room first. She could see that Troy wasn't in bed, and the bed hadn't been slept in. She continued down the hall; the door to Mya's room was slightly open, the television was on, and she could see her daughter on the bed asleep with her naked breast exposed. Her husband's masculine arms entwined her daughter's waist as they slept, spooning with each other. She could also see that Troy had no shirt on.

Teresa said, "For a minute, I just stood there. They looked so innocent and peaceful. I just knew this couldn't be what I thought. I was standing there trying to justify what I was seeing."

She pushed the door open and entered the room. Troy stirred first. He sat up, and the sheet fell away from his body; they were both totally nude. Troy looked at her like he had seen a ghost. He jumped out of bed and started running around the room. Teresa said she remembers that the closest thing to her was a trashcan, which she picked up and threw at her husband. The commotion woke Mya, who sat in bed, stunned.

Troy was running around the room screaming, "It's not how it looks!"

Teresa continued to throw anything she could reach as he ran from the room. He ran into their bedroom and locked the door. Mya was crying, Teresa grabbed her and demanded that she tell her what was going on. Teresa said her first instinct was to slap her daughter. She could hear the front door slam as Troy left. Then she sat there and held her daughter while they both cried. She was, after all, still just a baby, and this couldn't be her fault.

As she sat there, she could see what appeared to be dried cum stains on the sheets; she felt the bile rise in her throat. Teresa didn't know what to do or who to call. She had no other family nearby or anyone she could really call her friend. When she tried to find out from Mya just how long this had been going on, Mya only cried harder and refused to talk. Teresa did call the police to report the incident; however, she has no idea how she made it through the rest of the night. Troy never returned to the house, but he was eventually arrested.

The next day, Teresa called a therapist to schedule counseling for she and Mya. This was a long, difficult process. Mya was not cooperative, and it was later discovered during counseling that Mya didn't regard her stepfather as a father figure; she saw him as her man.

Ladies, please be extremely careful who you allow around your daughters. Never ignore warning signs. I realized after listening to Teresa's story that I was very fortunate. Ladies, talk to your daughters and let them know that although you are their parent, you are also a friend, and if they ever feel that they can't come to you with a problem, it is okay to talk to someone — a trusted friend or family member, even a teacher or someone within your church. Children don't know how to bring up such a delicate subject to anyone, not even a parent, so one of the best ways to protect your children is to make sure they know they have people to talk to when things just don't seem right.

Recognizing the Down-Low

When a man betrays his woman with another woman, it hurts. When a man chooses another *man* over his woman, it can be downright devastating. Yet, it is happening every day. More and more men are coming out of the closet and revealing their true sexuality.

There are more men living 'on the down-low' than you might think. For those of you who don't know what that means, let me break it down for you. A man who discreetly has sexual contact and/or intercourse with men, yet also has relationships with women, is considered to be on the down-low. They don't consider themselves gay or bisexual, and their female partners are not aware that they engage in sexual activity with other men. These men portray themselves as straight, yet they are not. Sadly, women are at a disadvantage because they don't know how to identify a man who may be living a down-low lifestyle.

Years ago, a man I had been dating exclusively for a few weeks began asking if we could experiment with anal sex. I have tried anal sex in the past, not because I was interested in it, but because my partners always seemed to have an interest in it. I found that it did nothing for me. I was not excited by it, nor was I turned on or in any way sexually stimulated by this act. It is important to not allow yourself to be talked into performing any sexual act that you are not comfortable with. If you don't enjoy something that a man is doing to you, just say so, because if you do allow it, your man will come to expect it, and you will eventually start to resent him when he asks you to engage in this act. It has been my experience that most men at some point suggest anal sex. As a woman, I can't even begin to tell you why it is so appealing to some men. Some men say it's adventurous, something different, a type of forbidden fruit. Most men don't even realize the magnitude of what they are asking you to do.

Over the years, I developed my own way of discouraging my sexual partner should he suggest we try this act and my way is this. I would say to my partner, "If I can go up in your anus with a dildo that is equivalent to your size, then I agree to let you do me." Now, as soon as you suggest this to most men, they will immediately change their minds and are no longer interested, but this one particular man said okay. I thought this was strange, but I wanted to see just how far he would go. We went to an adult bookstore and chose a ten-inch dildo (which was equivalent to his size), along with a couple of X-rated DVDs. We started our evening by going to dinner at one of my favorite exclusive restaurants. Along with the meal, we also had a few cocktails. Later, back at home, we popped in a DVD and got into a hot and heavy lovemaking session.

Ladies, I know it is a warning you've heard a hundred times, but it is worth being repeated here. Do not — under ANY circumstances — leave the responsibility up to a man to protect you sexually. Insist on using condoms every time. I could not begin to tell you how many women are infected with HIV or living with AIDS because they accepted a man's word. Do not become a statistic. Your life is worth more than his *or* your pleasure.

After we had done all the traditional stuff, he brought the subject up again about trying my forbidden sexual act. After making several unsuccessful attempts to work the dildo into his anus, I quickly became bored. I lost interest and began watching television. A few minutes later, my attention shifted back to the bed. Ladies, when you see a man on his hands and knees trying to shove a ten-inch dildo up his *own* ass, you really must think about what you're dealing with. This relationship eventually ended. I had trust issues, and he enjoyed spending time with the fellas a little too much. I'm not saying he was leading a down-low lifestyle, but you never know.

I later interviewed Keith, who, for all intents and purposes, was every woman's dream man. He was six-four, about 199 pounds, medium build, with abs to die for. He was sexy in *every* way, and he knew it. He was the type of man who walked past department store windows just to see his own reflection in the glass. Keith said he was in no way attracted to men, but he told me his story.

Once, he and his best boy, Miles, were hanging out at Miles' home watching the game. Miles was in a two-year committed relationship with his live-in girlfriend. He was also, by appearance, a heterosexual male. They were acting like guys, watching the game and drinking very heavily, starting with beer but ending up with the hard stuff. Keith said he fell asleep in the recliner, and when he woke up, the room was dark with the exception of the light from the television. On the screen was a sex scene.

Across the room, Miles was sitting on the sofa watching a sex flick. Miles, realizing that Keith was no longer asleep, said to him, "I hope you don't mind me watching this while you're here, man."

Keith answered, "It's your house. Go ahead and do your thing."

After a few minutes, Miles asked Keith, "Do you mind if I jack off?"

Keith admitted he was uncomfortable but said to him, "It's your house."

Miles took his penis out and started to stroke himself.

Keith, by this time also watching the flick, admitted to getting turned on, not by Miles' actions, but by the sex flick. He said, "Maybe it was the effects of the alcohol, but my boy asked if he could suck my dick. He said no one would ever have to know but us, so I let him." Keith's exact words were, "He sucked my shit so good, better than any woman ever has." But afterwards, he felt awkward whenever he was around Miles. He said, "To watch Miles with his girl, he's all man. If I hadn't had that experience with him, I never would have known there was a lot he was keeping on the down-low."

Of course I asked, "What about you? You allowed him to suck your dick."

Keith said, "Hell, I ain't no homo! I just wanted to get my dick sucked!" Keith says he and Miles continue to be boys, but they have never mentioned or repeated that night since.

I recognized that Keith was in denial, and by putting the blame on Miles for initiating their encounter, he could justify his part in the incident as being only a one-time thing — a moment of weakness.

Unfortunately, there is no way of knowing if your man is practicing a DL lifestyle until it is too late. You might already be married or in a long-term relationship with him, so naturally, you may no longer be using protection when you engage in sexual intercourse. This is why it is so important to be observant of your man prior to committing to that long-term relationship or marriage. This can sometimes be impossible to do because no matter how well you think you know someone, it is possible for a man to keep a secret like this for years before the truth is finally revealed. If you think your man is living on the down-low, you have a right to know about it for your own health and the health of your relationship.

The Beginning
(How to Build Self-Confidence)

When I was in high school, I was the ugly duckling. I was skinny and flat chested, with big lips and kinky hair. I was extremely self-conscious. I walked the halls with my head hung, and I wouldn't make eye contact with anyone. I wanted to draw the least amount of attention to myself as possible. My stepfather would playfully call me 'Olive Oyl' from the cartoon *Popeye.*

During my senior year, Anthony, one of the most popular guys in school, initiated a conversation with me. He said he wanted to get to know me and asked for my phone number. I remember thinking, *I'm not pretty. Why would he want my number?* I gave him my number, but I never expected him to actually call ... but he did, and every time he called, he did all the talking. He asked me questions about myself and wanted to know what my likes and dislikes were. He did everything to try and draw me into a conversation, but I was so shy and self-conscious that I didn't have anything to say to him.

After about a week of him trying to encourage me to open up and talk, he said, "I really like you. I think you are a beautiful girl, and you don't even know it. I can't get you to talk to me, and you'll only answer if I ask you a question, so I won't call you anymore because you're just too shy for me."

My response was, "Okay, bye." That was my senior year in high school. I never attended any school activities, and I didn't even go to my senior prom. I was just too shy to deal with guys, even though most guys seemed to actually like me.

I was nineteen years old when I lost my virginity to a twenty-six-year-old man I had met while I was attending community college. The funny thing was, this man didn't even attend the college. He was somewhat of a *predator*, someone who hangs out walking the halls trying to pick up college girls. I remember after sex with him the first time, I was left wondering, *Is this it? Is this what all the hype and hoopla is about? Hell, I make myself feel a lot better than this.* Fortunately, I later learned from someone else that things could get much better.

The following year, I joined the military, and that was one of the best decisions I ever made in my life. Not only did it teach me self-discipline, but it provided me with the opportunity to broaden my horizons by bringing me into contact with so many people in different countries with different cultures. The Army allowed me to experience things and people I might never have experienced on my own, as a result, I began to open up and be myself. During that time, I began to talk to men to see what caught their attention about women. More than I talked, I listened, honing in on their wants, needs, and desires. I even listened to some of them brag about their infidelities in relationships and why they felt the need and the right to cheat.

I also talked and listened to women, and I asked them the same questions I asked the men. Of course, I got very different answers from both. I began to discover that men and women have different needs and expectations from their relationships. What women consider to be issues, men view as unimportant.

As I was researching male/female relationships, I began to come out of my shell in a sort of transformation or transition period. I was still skinny and flat-chested with no butt, and I was still dreadfully shy, but I realized I had assets to offer, particularly full lips and shapely legs, which I had learned that men love. What I needed to work on was my self-esteem.

I learned to make eye contact with strangers, I began to flirt, and I began to voice my opinions, views, and ideas — not only to men, but to everyone I came in contact with. I learned to be heard, seen, and respected. I learned not to settle, and I came to the conclusion that there is always room for improvement in every-thing. However, sometimes it does not matter how much effort you put into improving yourself, for the fact still remains that all men are not attracted to the same thing. So, don't feel disappointed if that very attractive guy you just made eye contact with moves on by. He could be married, already involved in a rela-tionship, gay, or just not interested ... or maybe he just doesn't know a good thing when he sees it! There's no accounting for taste — or lack thereof!

Now, my friend, let's build basic self-confidence!!!

* Always start your day with a positive mental attitude. Positive energy is contagious. In my job as a casino table games dealer, I work directly with the public. I may be having a bad day, but I have learned to put my game face on. I project positive energy, and after a while, I actually start to feel positive.

* When you are out, make eye contact with the people you meet. Smile and say "Hello" not just to the men, but be cordial and friendly to everyone.

* Walk with your head held high, your shoulders back and take long, sure, comfortable strides. Remember that self-confidence is about attitude.

* Grooming is always important, as we've already discussed. Your hair should be neatly styled, clean, and fresh smelling; your nails should be manicured. One of my biggest pet peeves are run-down shoes, so keep your footwear in good condition. To determine the condition of your footwear, do the heel test. Place your shoes on a flat surface; if they don't stand straight, your heels have worn unevenly. Either have the shoes re-heeled or replace the shoes. Ladies, if you wear sandals or any shoe where most of your foot is exposed, don't overlook the condition of your feet. Nothing is less attractive than chipped toenail polish and calluses on your heels.

* Smile! Clean, healthy teeth are always attractive. How many times have you met someone and thought they were attractive until they smiled? Some things are common sense. If you have any obvious dental problems such as bleeding gums, cavities, or bad breath that won't go away after routine brushing, flossing, and rinsing, go see a dental care professional immediately. Remember, you only get one chance to make a first impression.

* Let your body language show that you are approachable. Always carry yourself well and maintain a positive self-image that demonstrates self-confidence and an approachable demeanor. Great relationships are built off chemistry. Chemistry is either there or it's not, but that shouldn't stop you from being nice to any man who approaches you in a respectful manner.

* Take care of your body. As I discussed earlier, always be clean and fresh.

* When a man approaches you, be yourself. Remember that differences make us who we are as individuals, and just because you may look, dress, or speak differently than someone else doesn't make you less important than the next person. Out of everything I taught myself, I continued to be me.

Once you have those things under control, it's time to take it to the next level!

How to Become a Sexually Desirable Woman
(Learning to Build Sexual Self-Confidence)

If there is one thing I am sure of, it's that you can learn to be a sexually desirable woman, even if you have never had success with men before. This chapter is designed to teach you how to be comfortable in your own skin. If you are one of the many women who can get your man, you may elect to skip over this chapter, but if you are one of the many women who lack self-esteem and are not confident enough to be outgoing and approachable, this chapter is for you.

This chapter is about self-discovery. In order to become a sexually desirable woman, you have to first discover who *you* are. A sexually desirable woman is not ashamed of her body; she is proud of it. She is not afraid to walk around nude in front of her man. She is confident, and it shows in everything she does. She is not afraid or ashamed to tell her man what she likes or to ask for what she wants.

I frequently hear from women who say that they hate to undress in front of their man because they have put on a few extra pounds, have stretch marks or their breasts have started to sag. There's not too much we can do about that, life happens. But as long as we do our best to keep ourselves together and try to maintain a healthy lifestyle the rest will take care of itself.

So ladies, let's get over it! Insecurities are normal, but hiding out from the one you love in your own home is not! One lady told me that she dreads going to bed at night because her husband insists on having sex with the lights on. She admitted that they frequently got into arguments most nights because she refuses to have sex with them on. I laughed and said to her, "If your man tells you he wants to *see* you make love to him that's one of the biggest compliments he can pay you." Ladies, it's true! My man *always* wants the lights on when we make love. Before we even get into it, I already know he's going to reach over and turn on the lamp so he can see. So in order to avoid him pulling away for that brief second during our love making session and interrupting *my* flow, I make it easy by turning the lights on before we ever get started. Let me explain something to you ladies, when your man is turned on and wants you he could care less about stretch marks or how much cellulite you have on your thighs. And the fact that you are open and carefree enough to experience intimacy with no inhibitions further excites him.

As I said, it is natural to suffer from insecurities. At some point in time, we all do. The first thing you must do in order to squash those doubts and insecurities is to learn yourself. Learn to get comfortable with your body and with your appearance.

Stand (nude) in front of a full-length mirror. It may sound crazy, but the objective is to familiarize yourself with your body. Study your appearance from every angle. Take note of your assets, your strong features, as well as your weaknesses. As I said earlier, all women have assets, and you have to discover what your assets are. You can't work with it if you don't know what you're working with. Lingerie can be your best friend IF you know how to select it. No matter what your body type is, there is a style designed to complement you. Being sexy is not about being someone else, but about enhancing you. It is too easy to disguise your flaws. For example, if your best features are your breasts and your worst is your stomach, select outfits that will expose your breast to your advantage while taking attention away from your stomach area. A corset or garter may slim your waistline surprisingly well. If your best features are your legs, dress in the outfit of your choice with a pair of sexy heels. If your best feature is your backside and your worst are your breasts, try a flattering bra; they come in all types of styles that are designed to give you what nature didn't. Be sure to highlight that wonderful backside by wearing a pair of matching thong panties.

Your wardrobe should contain a wide variety of lingerie, so go shopping! It is important to realize that selecting sexy lingerie can be a time-consuming endeavor. Don't think you will be able to walk into Victoria's Secret, grab up a few items, and expect the look that you are trying to achieve to just fall into place. Take your time when selecting your sexy attire, because you're worth it! In most cases, undergarments are non-returnable, so be sure to try your selections on before making purchases and leaving the store. You want your sexy garments to look good on you, but you also want to feel comfortable in them, so experiment with different styles and colors. After you bring the sexy garments home, wear them to get used to the feel of them against your body. Practice different poses to see how you look best. Take the time to really study your reflection. See what looks good on you. Look at yourself from your man's perspective.

High heels are the greatest invention ever created. No matter what your body type or what you wear, heels make you look sexy, and they accentuate your legs. If you are comfortable in your heels, they will give you poise and grace. I always wear heels, even if I'm home mopping the floor, cleaning, or doing the dishes! I started this habit years ago when I was going through a phase where I wasn't comfortable wearing heels. When I wanted to get dressed up in that sexy outfit, I felt clumsy and out of place because I just wasn't used to wearing heels. Now I am too comfortable in them, and it's just the opposite; I feel clumsy and out of place when I'm not in them ... and did I mention that my man loves to watch me clean house?

It is normal to feel awkward when you are trying out your new look for the first time in front of your man. If by this time you still don't feel totally confident with your appearance, try placing a few candles around the room to soften the lighting and create a more romantic atmosphere. Act casual. Walk around in your new underwear like it is the most natural thing on Earth. This is guaranteed to get your man's attention. Remember, sexuality is an attitude. You are totally in control. It's knowing that you are sexy that gives you power, so work it, girl!!!

Finding the Courage to Walk Away
(With your Dignity Intact)

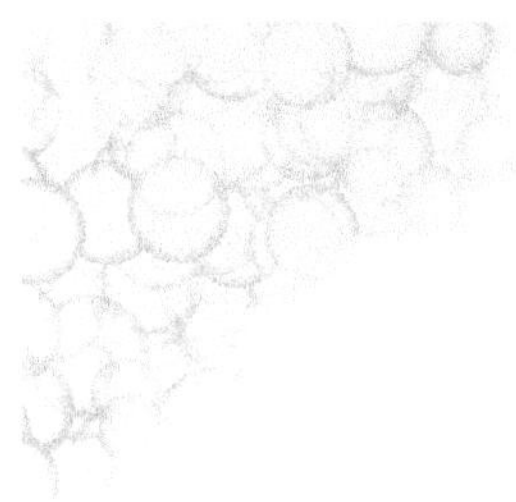

I have taken a lot of criticism from some people for having been married five times, but there is nothing I regret about my life. I look at my life as a necessary journey — one I had to take in order to become the woman I am today. Of course, I have made some mistakes along the way, but I like to consider them life lessons. I don't have to justify my reasons for my five previous marriages. I married five wonderful men, and they were each wonderful in their own way. Unfortunately, they also had other qualities that I could no longer live with.

We all know that busybody who loves to give their opinion about your relationship, so I never fail to tell those individuals to take their advice where it will do them the most good: home! No one can tell me what I should and should not put up with in my own home. I took each of my marriage vows seriously. I respected every relationship and put every effort into making my marriages successful, but sometimes you have to know when to cut your losses and move on. I learned that when it comes to being physically, verbally, or emotionally abused, you have to be strong enough to walk away. Never allow your fear of being labeled a failure to convince you to stay in a relationship that is not working on all levels. It is a far greater failure to stay in a destructive relationship than it is to find the courage to end it. Love yourself more than you love a man. When you walk away from a bad situation, you are saving yourself from future hurt and anguish. Yes, he will end up with someone else, but you should take comfort in the knowledge that he can do no more for the next woman than he did for you. Rest assured, he'll treat her the same or worse than he treated you, so you are better off without him.

I truly believe no one has to tell you when someone is no good for you, but sometimes we look for all the wrong reasons to make a bad situation work. The best thing is to call it quits if the man you are seeing is not giving you the love and respect you deserve. The man in my life must complement my existence. He must add to the experience of living, not take away from it. You don't need stress, attitude, or drama, and you should never have to fight for time and attention.

When a man cares for you and wants to be with you, respect alone will make him *want* to include you. On his own, he'll pick up the phone and say, "Baby, this is where I am," because he'll want you to be part of every facet of his life, and you'll never have to waste hours watching the clock, wondering where your man is. We only have one life, and when it's gone, it's gone. We can waste it with men who contribute nothing positive to our existence, or we can open our eyes and start to recognize when men don't have the same values, morals, and principles that we have and walk away. Why waste one minute of our precious life? Look in the mirror; the reflection staring back at you won't be the same in ten years. We should embrace and enjoy every moment of living and capture the beauty of life before it is all over.

What Is Therapy?

herapy is the importance of teaching women to love themselves so that when dealing with negative issues associated with men, love, and relationships, we know the importance of healing.

Therapy is knowing that when men lie, cheat, and leave, it is not your fault. When you love yourself — truly love yourself — you will be able to recognize and accept when someone truly loves you. I had to know each and every time I ended a relationship that I love myself. I love myself too much to settle for what I was getting. I deserved more — not more material things, possessions, or money, but I deserved to be loved and cherished in return.

Therapy is when you take the time to separate yourself from the situation and work on healing and self-love so that you don't carry the same baggage into your next relationship. When you come out of a relationship better and smarter than when you went in, you've found true *therapy*.

The Common Bonds of Sisterhood
(A Message for my Sisters)

Throughout our lifetime women have and will face many challenges in life. Your challenges may not be like mine, but we do share a common thread. In many ways we are all the same woman, although we may be separated by age, race, religion, and culture; women share many common traits. You might look at your life and feel like you are all messed up. You might look in the mirror and not like the person you see looking back at you. We carry old wounds and we are emotionally scarred by our issues in life — abusive relationships, rape, molestation, incest, lack of love and affection from our parents and the list goes on. Many of us haven't healed, but we try to hide those open wounds by continuing to cover them with bandages. We put up this façade to the world as if everything is okay. We pretend to be normal, when on the inside we're anything *but* normal. We have to find a way to heal. Many women have tried counseling, and some women have found it to be helpful in getting them to come to terms with their issues, but in some cases it didn't help them *heal*. Even after counseling many women continue to carry the anguish and pain of their past throughout their lives.

How can you heal the pain? In order for some wounds to heal it needs air, it needs to breathe, and when you cover a wound with bandages it can't breathe. So we have to rip those bandages off and let our wounds breathe, so they can begin to heal. One way to heal is to stop acting like it never happened. Reach out to other women, talk about it; realize that no matter what has happened in your past you deserve goodness in your life. Let's stop being so critical of the next woman. Let's stop judging each other and accept that we've all had to make some difficult decisions in life and sometime maybe it wasn't the right decision. There is a saying that goes: "When we learn better we do better." Every experience brought into your life, whether good or bad, plays a critical role in your personal growth and development. Welcome those experiences, for they were meant to teach you about yourself.

Many young women reach out to me on a daily basis who are troubled by issues of their past and although I may not agree with some of the decisions these young ladies have made, I don't judge, all I can do is encourage her and love her like a sister. Showing love for my sisters helps me to heal. I also find my healing in letting go of any situation that causes me grief and letting God handle it. It works for me, I know if you give Him a try it can work for you too! Remember ladies, one of the most important relationships you will *ever* have is the one you have with yourself.

WHY I WROTE THIS BOOK

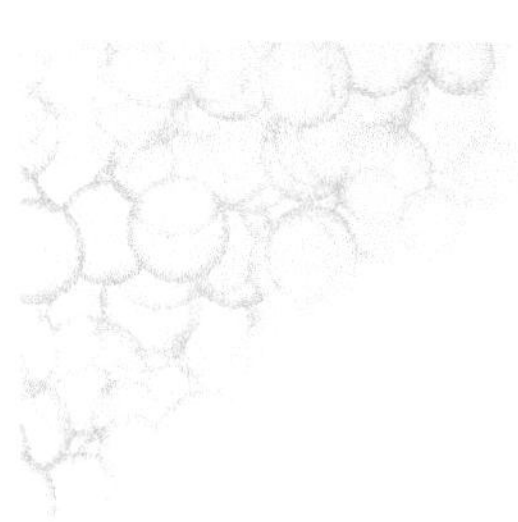

During all the relationships throughout my life, I put my man's needs before my own. Like many women do, I bent over backwards to make sure *he* was happy and that *his* needs were met, but in the process, I forgot about me and my needs.

Over the years, I realized that I wasn't the only woman letting her man's needs consume her. I realized that all women need to take time out to pamper, nurture and love ourselves, just as we do our men. If we spend some time loving ourselves, we will be better mothers, lovers, nurturers, and overall partners for our men.

Now, although I still 'take care of my man', I also make it a priority of taking care of myself. It is my hope that the information in this book can teach other women that there is a way to take care of the man we love, while also taking care of ourselves ... and that is just the kind of therapy we all need.

About the Author

Glenda Wallace is the Founder & CEO of Pink Kiss Publishing Company. She is an author, entrepreneur, educator and creative consultant. She is also the host of the 'real' talk internet radio show "The G-Spot" on Blog Talk Radio.

Ms. Wallace is dedicated to uplifting, inspiring and empowering women to discover their true potential so that they may achieve the highest level of success. She lives, works and plays on the MS Gulf Coast.

Please visit her website @
www.pinkkisspublishing.com

tionship with yourself, your significant other and those around you to a whole new level.

If you only buy one relationship book in your life, you should make this the one. It is sure to be one of the best investments you ever make.

Order your copy today at http://www.pinkkisspublishing.com/Order-Page.html

ISBN#978-0-615-29068-3
$10.95 US/free shipping

Available from your favorite bookseller!